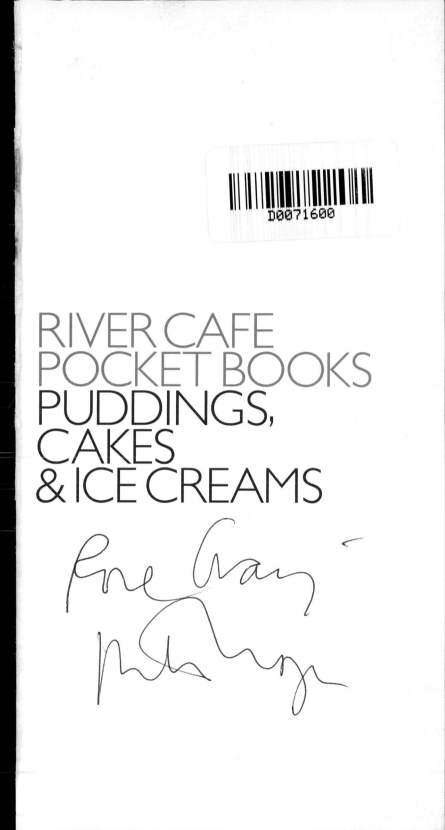

D0071600

RIVER CAFE
POCKET BOOKS
PUDDINGS,
CAKES
& ICE CREAMS

RIVER CAFE
POCKET BOOKS
PUDDINGS,
CAKES
& ICE CREAMS

ROSE GRAY AND RUTH ROGERS

Introduction

Index

Introduction

The puddings in this book span the 19 years we have been cooking in the River Cafe, from the almond tart that was on the menu the first day we opened, to the delicious lemon and ricotta cake we discovered in Tuscany just last summer.

Like all the food we cook, the puddings we've chosen are both seasonal and regional. Lovely recipes, such as the lemon apple tart and the Vernazza cake, were taught to us by chefs and friends when visiting Italy. Others have evolved as our tastes developed, sometimes Italianising traditional English recipes such as Summer pudding, by using sourdough bread, or accompanying the classic Italian panna cotta with champagne rhubarb and orange peel.

The puddings in this book are quick and easy to make. We use an electric mixer to beat the eggs and sugar, and suggest you invest in a good set of scales. When making the cakes, as ovens differ, use your own judgement as well as our guidance. Feel the top of the cake to test for firmness, or insert a skewer to see if the cake is cooked inside.

Though in our first River Cafe Cookbook we wrote that Italians tend to have their cakes for breakfast and prefer to end a meal simply with an espresso, we also know that nearly everyone looks forward to eating a mouth-watering dessert.

All recipes serve four unless otherwise stated. The quantities we have given for 10 will give you ice creams and sorbets just as delicious if divided in half. All eggs are medium, free-range, organic unless otherwise stated.

CHAPTER ONE
TARTS

1   Sweet pastry tart shell

Serves 14

350g Plain flour • A pinch of salt • 125g Cold unsalted butter, cut into cubes • 100g Icing sugar • 3 Large egg yolks

Preheat the oven to 180°C/Gas Mark 4.

Pulse the flour, salt and butter in a food processor until the mixture resembles coarse breadcrumbs. Add the sugar, then the egg yolks, and pulse again. The mixture will immediately combine and leave the sides of the bowl. Remove, form into a ball, wrap in cling film and chill for at least an hour.

Using the large holes in the side of a cheese grater, coarsely grate the pastry into a 30cm loose-bottomed fluted flan tin, then press it evenly onto the sides and the base. Prick the base with a fork and chill for at least 10 minutes. Bake blind for 20 minutes, until very light brown. Cool and remove from the tin.

2   Blackberry and almond tart

Serves 14

750g Blackberries • 350g Almonds, finely ground • 350g Caster sugar • 1 Vanilla pod, split in half, seeds scraped out • 350g Unsalted butter, softened • 50g Icing sugar • 4 Eggs • 1 Sweet Pastry Tart Shell (see Recipe 1), baked and cooled

Preheat the oven to 150°C/Gas Mark 2.

Mix the caster sugar with the vanilla seeds. Using an electric mixer, beat the butter and sugar together until pale and light. Add the ground almonds and blend, then beat in the eggs one by one. Pour into the tart shell and bake for 45 minutes.

Cool, remove from the tin and cover with blackberries. Sieve over the icing sugar just before serving.

3 Raspberry and almond tart

Serves 14

750g Raspberries • 350g Almonds, finely ground • 350g Unsalted butter, softened • 350g Caster sugar • 4 Large eggs • 1 Sweet Pastry Tart Shell (see Recipe 1), baked and cooled

Preheat the oven to 150°C/Gas Mark 2.

Using an electric mixer, beat the butter and sugar together until pale and light. Add the ground almonds and blend, then beat in the eggs one by one. Pour into the tart shell and bake for 45 minutes. Cool, remove from the tin and cover with raspberries.

If the raspberries are sour top with 1 tbs of caster sugar before scattering over the tart.

Raspberry and almond tart (Recipe 3)

4   Pear and almond tart

Serves 14

4 Ripe Comice pears, peeled, halved and cored • 300g Almonds, finely ground • 1 Sweet Pastry Tart Shell (see Recipe 1), baked and cooled • 300g Unsalted butter, softened • 300g Caster sugar • 3 Large eggs • Crème fraîche, to serve

Preheat the oven to 150°C/Gas Mark 2. Place the pears face down in the tart shell.

Using an electric mixer, beat the butter and sugar together until pale and light. Add the ground almonds and blend, then beat in the eggs one by one. Pour the mixture over the pears and bake for 45 minutes. Cool and remove from the tin. Serve with crème fraîche.

5   Plum, Amaretto and almond tart

Serves 14

500g Dark-skinned plums, halved and stoned • 100ml Amaretto liqueur • 300g Almonds, finely ground • 300g Unsalted butter, softened • 300g Caster sugar • 3 Large eggs • 1 Sweet Pastry Tart Shell (see Recipe 1), baked and cooled

Preheat the oven to 150°C/Gas Mark 2.

Using an electric mixer, beat the butter and sugar together until pale and light. Add the ground almonds, blend to combine, then add the eggs, one by one. Finally, slowly add the Amaretto.

Pour this mixture into the tart shell. Push the plums, cut-side up, into the filling and bake in the preheated oven for 45 minutes. Cool and remove from the tin.

6 Prune and almond tart

Serves 14

16 Prunes d'Agen, stoned • 300g Almonds, finely ground • 1 Earl Grey teabag • 100ml Vecchio Romagna brandy • 300g Unsalted butter, softened • 300g Caster sugar • 3 Large eggs • 1 Sweet Pastry Tart Shell (see Recipe 1), baked and cooled

Preheat the oven to 150°C/Gas Mark 2.

Pour enough boiling water over the prunes to cover, then add the teabag. Leave to expand for 1 hour. Remove the prunes from the water and pour the brandy over them.

Using an electric mixer, beat the butter and sugar together until pale and light. Add the ground almonds, blend to combine, then add the eggs, one by one. Finally add the brandy prune juices.

Pour this mixture into the tart shell. Push the prunes into the mixture. Bake in the preheated oven for 40 minutes. Cool and remove from the tin.

Prune and almond tart (Recipe 6)

7   Apricot, lemon almond tart

Serves 14

*500g Fresh ripe apricots, halved and stoned •
Juice and finely grated zest of 1 lemon • 300g
Almonds, finely ground • 300g Unsalted butter,
softened • 300g Caster sugar • 3 Large eggs • 1
Sweet Pastry Tart Shell (see Recipe 1), baked and
cooled*

Preheat the oven to 150°C/Gas Mark 2.

Using an electric mixer, cream the butter and sugar
together until pale and light. Add the almonds, blend,
then slowly add the grated lemon zest and lemon
juice. Beat in the eggs, one by one. Pour the filling into
the tart shell. Push the apricots into the mixture.

Bake in the preheated oven for 40 minutes. Cool and
remove from the tin.

8   Lemon, mascarpone tart

Serves 14

*Juice and grated zest of 6 lemons • 300g
Mascarpone • 6 Eggs • 6 Egg yolks • 350g Caster
sugar • 1 Sweet Pastry Tart Shell (see Recipe 1), baked
and cooled • 2 tbs Icing sugar*

Preheat the oven to 140°C/Gas Mark 1.

In a bowl combine the lemon juice and zest. Beat the eggs and yolks with the sugar until pale. Fold in the mascarpone and combine, then fold in the lemon mixture. Pour into the tart shell and bake for 1 hour. When cool, sprinkle over the icing sugar and remove from the tin.

9 Lemon tart

Serves 14

Grated zest and juice of 4 lemons • 350g Caster sugar • 6 Eggs • 9 Egg yolks • 300g Unsalted butter, softened • 1 Sweet Pastry Tart Shell (see Recipe 1), baked and cooled

Preheat the oven to 230°C/Gas Mark 8.

Put the lemon zest and juice, sugar, eggs and yolks in a large saucepan over a very low heat. Whisk until the eggs have broken up and the sugar has dissolved. Add half the butter and continue to whisk. At this point the eggs will start to cook and the mixture will thicken enough to coat the back of a spoon. Add the remaining butter and continue whisking until the mixture becomes very thick. It is important to continue whisking throughout the cooking process to prevent the mixture curdling. Remove from the heat, place on a cold surface and continue to whisk until lukewarm.

Spoon the lemon filling into the tart shell and bake until the top is brown. This should take about 5-8 minutes. Cool and remove from the tin.

Lemon tart (Recipe 9)

10 Cherry focaccia

Serves 14

1kg Cherries, stoned • 1 tsp Dried yeast • 350ml Warm water • 500g Plain flour • 100g Caster sugar • Extra virgin olive oil

In a warm bowl, mix the yeast with the warm water, then let it rest for 5 minutes. Gently pour in the flour and stir to combine (the dough should be very soft). Then slowly mix in 50ml olive oil along with half the sugar and a pinch of salt. Knead on a floured work surface for 5 minutes. Return to the bowl, cover with a cloth and set aside to rise for an hour or until doubled in size.

When the dough has risen, roll it out and place on a lightly oiled pizza pan, 30cm in diameter. Place the cherries over the dough and let it rise again for half an hour. Preheat the oven to 180°C/Gas Mark 4.

Sprinkle the remaining sugar over the cake and drizzle with a small amount of olive oil. Place in the oven and bake for about 30 minutes, until brown. Serve warm or at room temperature.

11   Lemon apple tart

Grated zest of 2 lemons • 4 Large or 8 small sour apples, peeled, cored and finely sliced • 110g Butter • 300g Caster sugar, plus 2 tbs • 1 Vanilla pod, split in half, seeds scraped out • 3 Eggs • 150ml Milk • 125g Blanched almonds, finely ground • 6 tbs Plain flour • 2 tsp Baking powder

Preheat the oven to 150°C/Gas Mark 2.

Line a 23cm tart tin with baking parchment and grease with extra butter.

Melt the butter. Mix the 300g of caster sugar with the vanilla seeds.

Beat the vanilla sugar and the eggs together until thick and light. Add the lemon zest. Slowly add the milk and melted butter. Mix the almonds into the plain flour. Add the baking powder and then stir this into the egg and sugar mixture.

Pour half the batter into the prepared tin, cover with half the apples and scatter with 1 tbs of caster sugar. Cover with the remaining batter and then cover with the remaining apples. Scatter over the remaining 1 tbs of caster sugar.

Bake in the oven for 45 minutes-1 hour. Cool and remove from the tin.

Lemon apple tart (Recipe 11)

CHAPTER
TWO
CAKES

12 Chocolate espresso and hazelnut cake

Serves 8

180g 70% Chocolate, broken into small pieces • 4 tbs Instant coffee • 480g Shelled hazelnuts • 300g Unsalted butter • 6 Eggs, separated • 220g Caster sugar

Preheat the oven to 150°C/Gas Mark 2. Butter a 25cm round cake tin and line it with baking parchment.

To roast the hazelnuts, spread them out on an oven tray and place in an oven preheated to 150°C/Gas Mark 2 until their skins become crisp and the nuts begin to colour, about 20 minutes. Place the hot nuts in a tea towel, fold it over and rub them on a flat surface in the towel. This will remove the skins.

Place the hazelnuts in a food processor and grind to a fine powder.

Dissolve the instant coffee in 1 tbs of hot water. Melt the chocolate with the butter and coffee in a bowl set over a pan of simmering water. Do not let the water touch the bowl. Cool, then fold in the hazelnuts.

Using an electric mixer, beat the egg yolks and sugar until pale and doubled in size. Fold in the chocolate mixture. Beat the egg whites until stiff and then carefully fold into the mixture. Pour into the tin. Bake in the oven for 40 minutes. Remove from the tin when completely cool.

13 Bitter chocolate roasted hazelnut cake

Serves 10

500g 70% Chocolate, broken into small pieces • 500g Shelled hazelnuts, roasted, skins rubbed off (see Recipe 12) • 500g Unsalted butter, softened • 500g Caster sugar • 12 Eggs

Preheat the oven to 150°C/Gas Mark 2. Butter a 30cm round cake tin, and line it with baking parchment.

Place the hazelnuts in a food processor and pulse-chop to a rough texture.

Place the chocolate in a bowl set over a pan of simmering water and leave to melt. Do not stir.

Using an electric mixer, beat the butter with the sugar until light. Slowly add the liquid chocolate, allowing it to blend in. Add the eggs, one by one, continuing to mix gently. When all the eggs are incorporated, fold in the nuts.

Pour the mixture into the prepared cake tin and bake for 40-50 minutes. Test for doneness with a skewer – it should come out dry. Turn off the oven but leave the cake in it, with the door slightly ajar, for a further 30 minutes. Remove from the tin when completely cool.

14 Chocolate, walnut brandy cake

Serves 8

250g 70% Chocolate, broken into small pieces • 300g Walnuts, finely chopped • 3 tbs Brandy • 350g Unsalted butter • 4 Eggs, separated • 220g Caster sugar

Preheat the oven to 160°C/Gas Mark 3. Butter a 25cm round cake tin and line it with baking parchment.

Melt the chocolate with the butter in a bowl set over a pan of simmering water. Do not let the water touch the bowl.

Using an electric mixer, beat the egg yolks with the sugar until pale and light. Slowly add the melted chocolate, then fold in the walnuts. Beat the egg whites until stiff and fold into the mixture. Pour into the tin.

Bake for 10 minutes. Reduce the heat to 150°C/Gas Mark 2 and bake for a further 45 minutes. Cool in the tin. When cool, turn out and pour the brandy over the cake.

15   Chocolate and ginger cake

Serves 12

500g 70% Chocolate • 200g Fresh root ginger, peeled and finely chopped • 500g Unsalted butter • 70g Fine polenta flour • 2 tbs Cocoa powder • 10 Eggs • 400g Caster sugar • 1/4 tsp Baking powder • Crème fraîche, to serve

Preheat the oven to 150°C/Gas Mark 2. Butter a 30cm round springform cake tin and line it with baking parchment.

Melt the chocolate and butter together in a bowl set over a pan of simmering water. Do not let the bowl touch the water. Add the ginger to the chocolate mixture once it has melted, along with the polenta and cocoa powder. Allow to cool.

Using an electric mixer, beat the eggs and sugar together until they have trebled in volume. Fold the mixture into the chocolate, along with the baking powder. Pour into the tin and bake for 45 minutes, then remove from the oven. Cover with a piece of baking parchment and place a plate on top of the cake until cool. Remove the plate and parchment and serve with crème fraîche.

16 Torta caprese

Serves 8

*225g Unsalted butter, softened • 225g Sugar •
6 Large eggs, separated • 225g Almonds, coarsely
ground •225g Bitter 100% chocolate, coarsely ground
in a food processor*

Preheat the oven to 150°C/Gas Mark 2. Butter a
25cm round, deep springform cake tin and line the
bottom with baking parchment.

Using an electric mixer, beat the butter and sugar
together until pale and light. Add the egg yolks, one by
one, then the almonds and chocolate.

Beat the egg whites separately until they form soft
peaks. Fold about a quarter into the stiff chocolate
mixture to loosen it a little, then fold this mixture into
the remaining egg whites.

Pour into the prepared cake tin and bake for 45
minutes, until set. Test by inserting a skewer; if the
torta is cooked, it will come out clean.

17 Fifteen-minute chocolate cake

Serves 8

*450g 70% Chocolate, broken into small pieces •
200g Unsalted butter • 6 Eggs*

Preheat the oven to 220°C/Gas Mark 7. Butter a
25cm round cake tin and line it with baking
parchment.

Melt the chocolate with the butter in a bowl placed
over a pan of simmering water. The water should not
touch the bowl. In a separate bowl, over simmering
water, beat the eggs with an electric whisk until they
start to thicken, then remove from the heat and
continue beating until firm peaks form.

Fold half the eggs into the melted chocolate, then fold
in the remainder. Pour the mixture into the tin and
cover with buttered foil.

Put a folded kitchen cloth in the bottom of a deep
baking tray. Put in the cake tin and add enough very
hot water to come halfway up the side of the tin; this
is essential if the cake is to cook evenly. Place in the
oven and bake for 5 minutes, then remove the foil and
bake for a further 10 minutes, until just set. Remove
from the water and cool in the tin. Turn out when
completely cool.

18 Hazelnut truffle cake

Serves 8

200g Shelled hazelnuts, roasted, skins rubbed off (see Recipe 12) • 120g Unsalted butter • 6 tbs Demerara sugar • 250g 70% Chocolate, broken into small pieces • 150ml Dark rum • 4 Egg yolks • 250ml Double cream

Preheat the oven to 150°C/Gas Mark 2. Butter the base of a 16cm round springform cake tin. Line with baking parchment and butter the paper.

Pulse-chop the hazelnuts in a food processor until finely ground. Melt the butter in a small, thick-bottomed saucepan, add the sugar and boil until lightly caramelised. Add the hazelnuts and stir until they begin to stick together, about 2-3 minutes. Whilst it is still warm, spread this mixture over the base of the prepared tin.

Melt the chocolate with the rum in a bowl set over a pan of simmering water, making sure the water does not touch the base of the bowl. Cool. Beat the egg yolks until pale. Stir them into the chocolate, then slowly add the cream. The mixture will thicken immediately. Spoon it into the cake tin and leave to set for 1 hour in the fridge.

To remove the cake from the tin, soak a cloth in hot water and wrap it around the tin for 1 minute to melt the edges slightly. Unclip the springform. Carefully slide the cake off the base onto a plate.

19   Pressed chocolate cake

Serves 8

*400g 70% Chocolate, broken into small pieces •
300g Unsalted butter • Flour for dusting • 10 Eggs,
separated • 225g Caster sugar • 4 tbs Cocoa powder*

Preheat the oven to 180°C/Gas Mark 4. Butter and
flour a 25cm round cake tin, 7cm deep.

Melt the chocolate with the butter in a bowl set over
a pan of simmering water. The water should not touch
the bowl. Remove the bowl from the pan and cool a
little. Whisk the egg yolks with the sugar until pale and
thick. Stir gently into the cooled chocolate mixture.
Fold in the cocoa powder.

Beat the egg whites until they form soft peaks. Fold
into the chocolate mixture, ⅓ at a time. Pour the
mixture into the prepared tin and bake for
approximately 30 minutes, until the cake has risen like
a soufflé and is slightly set. Place a plate on top that
fits within 1cm inside the cake tin. Press firmly down
and put a weight on top of it to squash the cake and
allow the edges to erupt over the side. Leave to cool
before turning out.

Pressed chocolate cake (Recipe 19)

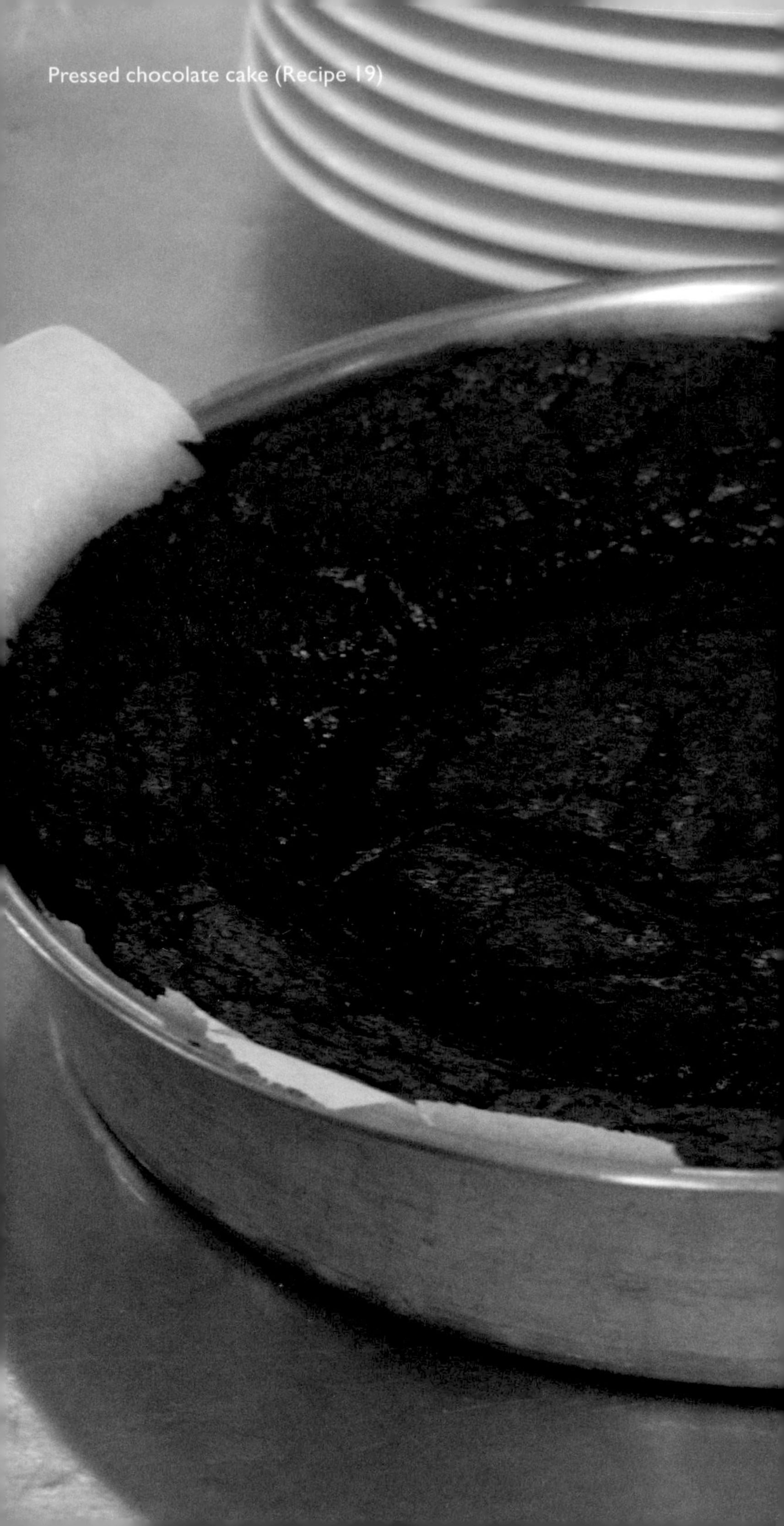

Pressed chocolate cake (Recipe 19)

20   Easy chocolate nemesis

Serves 8

340g 70% Chocolate, broken into small pieces • 225g Unsalted butter • 5 Eggs • 210g Caster sugar

Preheat the oven to 120°C/Gas Mark ½. Butter a 25cm round cake tin and line it with baking parchment.

Melt the chocolate with the butter in a bowl set over a pan of simmering water. Do not let the water touch the bowl. Beat the eggs with 70g of the sugar in an electric mixer until the mixture quadruples in volume.

Heat the remaining sugar with 100ml water until dissolved. Let it boil for a minute or so until it forms a light syrup. Pour the hot syrup into the melted chocolate and cool slightly. Add the chocolate to the eggs and beat slowly until the mixture is combined. Pour into the prepared tin.

Put a folded kitchen cloth in the bottom of a deep baking tray. Put in the cake and add enough hot water to come three-quarters of the way up the side of the tin. Bake for 50 minutes, until set. Leave the cake to cool in the water before turning out.

21 Rum and coffee truffle cake

Serves 6

200ml Rum • 3 tbs Instant coffee • 500g 70% Chocolate, broken into small pieces • 600ml Double cream • 3 tbs Cocoa powder

Melt the chocolate in a bowl over a pan of hot water. Do not stir. Warm the cream, dissolve the instant coffee into it and mix with the rum and melted chocolate. Place a 15cm cake ring on a plate, pour the mixture into the ring and put in the fridge for 2 hours.

To remove the ring, soak a cloth in hot water and wrap around the ring for 2 minutes to melt the edges of the cake. Pull off the ring carefully and shake the cocoa powder over the top.

Rum and coffee truffle cake (Recipe 21)

22 Dark truffle cake

Serves 6

225g 70% Chocolate, broken into small pieces •
300ml Double cream • 2 tbs Cocoa powder

Melt the chocolate in a bowl set over a pan of hot water. Do not stir. Warm the cream, then stir it into the melted chocolate. Place a 15cm cake ring on a plate, pour the mixture into the ring and put in the fridge for 2 hours.

To remove the ring, soak a cloth in hot water and wrap around the ring for 2 minutes to melt the edges of the cake, making it easy to turn out. Shake the cocoa powder over the top.

23 Bitter chocolate mousse cake

Serves 8

Sponge
100g Unsalted butter, softened • 100g Plain flour •
100g Caster sugar • 2 Eggs • 2 tsp Baking powder

Chocolate mousse
175g 70% Chocolate, broken into small pieces •
4 Eggs, separated • 115g Caster sugar • 3 tbs Strong coffee • 175g Unsalted butter

To serve
80ml Brandy • 150ml Double cream • 1 tbs Cocoa powder

Preheat the oven to 150°C/Gas Mark 2. Butter and flour a 22.5 x 11cm loaf tin.

For the sponge, cream the butter and sugar together until pale. Beat in the eggs, one at a time. Fold in the flour and baking powder and put into the prepared tin. Bake for 15 minutes. Turn out onto a rack to cool.

For the mousse, beat the egg yolks with 100g of the sugar until pale, about 5 minutes. Melt the chocolate with the coffee in a bowl set over a pan of simmering water, making sure the water does not touch the bowl. Remove from the heat and stir in the butter, a little at a time. Add to the egg mixture.

Beat the egg whites to soft peaks. Add the remaining sugar and beat until stiff. Fold them into the chocolate, then cover and chill for at least 2 hours.

Cut the sponge into horizontal slices 1cm thick. Line the bottom of the loaf tin with baking parchment and cover with a single layer of sponge. Drizzle with half the brandy and spoon in a layer of mousse. Line the sides of the tin with slices of sponge and fill with the remaining mousse.

Cover with sponge, drizzle with the remaining brandy and press down. Chill for 1 hour.

Unmould the cake from the tin and place on a serving plate. Whip the cream, spread it over the cake and shake over the cocoa powder.

24 Hazelnut meringue cake

Serves 10

Chocolate mousse
450g 70% Chocolate • 2 tbs Instant coffee, dissolved in 80ml boiling water • 6 Eggs, separated • Sea salt

Meringue
150g Shelled hazelnuts, roasted, skins rubbed off (see Recipe 12) • Olive oil and butter for greasing • 5 Egg whites • 225g Caster sugar • 110g Unsalted butter, melted • 70g Plain flour

To serve
100ml Brandy • 200g Mascarpone, whipped

For the mousse, melt the chocolate in a bowl with the coffee over a saucepan of simmering water. Do not let the water touch the bowl.

Using an electric mixer, beat the egg yolks until pale and light. Gradually add the melted chocolate mixture. In a separate bowl, beat the egg whites with the salt to soft peaks. Fold a large spoonful of egg white into the chocolate mixture, then fold in a further spoonful to combine. Finally fold the remaining egg whites into the chocolate. Cover with cling film and leave in the fridge overnight.

For the meringue, preheat the oven to 120°C/Gas Mark ½. Rub olive oil over 3 flat oven trays. Line each tray with baking parchment and generously butter the paper.

Put the hazelnuts in a food processor and pulse-chop to a medium-fine flour.

Beat the egg whites with half the sugar until stiff, then add the hazelnut flour and the remaining sugar. Beat briefly just to combine. Fold in the melted butter. Sift the flour into the bowl and fold in carefully.

Spoon the mixture onto the 3 trays and spread it out flat, each the same shape and diameter, but as thin as possible. The layers should be 1 cm thick at most.

Place in the preheated oven and bake for 50 minutes, or until set and almost crisp. Immediately peel off the paper whilst the meringues are still hot. Place on wire racks to cool.

To assemble the cake, choose a large, flat serving plate. Divide the chocolate mousse mixture in half. Place the first meringue layer on the plate, sprinkle over half the brandy and let it soak in. Cover with a thick layer of the chocolate mousse. Place the second meringue on top, sprinkle with the remaining brandy and spread with the remaining mousse. Sit the last meringue on top and cover with the mascarpone.

25 Pear, honey and polenta cake

Serves 8

*850g Pears, peeled, cored and cut into 2cm dice •
40g Runny honey • 115g Polenta • 320g Unsalted
butter • 225g Caster sugar • 3 Eggs • 115g Almonds,
finely ground • 35g Plain flour • 1 tsp Baking powder •
Grated zest of 2 lemons*

Preheat the oven to 150°C/Gas Mark 2. Line a 22 ×
12cm loaf tin, 6cm deep, with baking parchment, then
butter it.

Melt 80g of the butter in a non-stick saucepan, add
the honey and cook briefly until caramelised. Add the
pears and turn them to coat.

Beat the remaining butter with the sugar until light
and fluffy. Beat in the eggs, one by one. Mix the
almonds with the polenta, plain flour and baking
powder and fold into the butter and egg mixture.
Carefully fold in the warm pears and honey, along
with the lemon zest. Gently spoon the mixture into
the prepared cake tin and bake for 1¼-1½ hours.
The cake will be quite dark on top and should be firm
when pressed.

26 Polenta, lemon almond cake

Serves 10

*225g Polenta • Grated zest of 4 lemons • Juice of
1 lemon • 450g Almonds, ground • 450g Unsalted*

butter, softened • Flour for dusting • 450g Caster sugar • 2 tsp Vanilla extract • 6 Eggs • 1 tsp Baking powder • ½ tsp Salt

Preheat the oven to 160°C/Gas Mark 3. Butter and flour a 30cm round cake tin.

Using an electric mixer, beat the butter and sugar together until pale and light. Stir in the ground almonds and vanilla. Beat in the eggs, one at a time. Fold in the lemon zest and juice, polenta, baking powder and salt.

Spoon into the prepared tin and bake in the preheated oven for 45 minutes or until set. The cake will be brown on top. Serve with crème fraîche.

27 Polenta crumble

Serves 6

140g Polenta • Grated zest of 1 lemon • 120g Blanched almonds, coarsely ground • 120g Plain flour • 120g Caster sugar • 2 Egg yolks • 120g Unsalted butter, softened

Preheat the oven to 180°C/Gas Mark 4. Butter and flour a 20cm round cake tin.

Put the lemon zest and almonds in a bowl with the flour, polenta and sugar. With a fork, mix in the egg yolks, then the butter. You should have a crumbly dough. Press this dough into the prepared tin. Bake for 30 minutes. Allow to cool completely before cutting.

Polenta crumble (Recipe 27)

28 Lemon and almond cake

Serves 6

Juice and grated zest of 4 lemons • 300g Almonds, finely ground • 200g Caster sugar • 5 Egg yolks • 150g Unsalted butter, softened • 100g Self-raising flour • 3 Egg whites • 2 tsp Baking powder

Preheat the oven to 180°C/Gas Mark 4. Butter and flour a 25cm cake tin.

Put the lemon juice and zest in a saucepan and add the sugar and egg yolks. Cook gently, stirring, over a very low heat until thick. Stir in the butter in small amounts. Strain through muslin and cool.

Add the ground almonds and flour to the lemon mixture. Beat the egg whites to soft peaks. Fold in the baking powder and then combine with the lemon and almond mixture. Pour into the prepared tin and bake in the preheated oven for 50 minutes. Allow to cool in the tin.

29 Walnut and almond cake

Serves 6-8

200g Walnuts, finely chopped • 380g Almonds, finely ground • 380g Unsalted butter, softened • 380g Caster sugar • 3 Vanilla pods, very finely chopped • 5 Eggs • 100g Plain flour • ½ tsp Baking powder • 125ml Amaretto liqueur

Icing
200g 70% Chocolate, broken into small pieces • 50g
Unsalted butter

Preheat the oven to 160°C/Gas Mark 3. Butter and flour a 25cm round cake tin.

Using an electric mixer, beat the butter and sugar together until light. Stir in the almonds and vanilla pods. Beat in the eggs, one at a time. Fold in the walnuts, flour, baking powder and finally the Amaretto. Spoon into the tin and bake for 1 ¼ hours or until set. Turn out of the tin onto a wire rack and leave to cool.

Melt the chocolate and butter in a bowl set over a pan of simmering water. The water should not touch the bowl. Spread the mixture over the cake, using a hot, wet knife.

---

30 Pine nut loaf cake

Serves 6

6 tbs Pine nuts • 250g Unsalted butter, softened •
220g Caster sugar • Seeds from 2 vanilla pods •
4 Eggs • 100g Plain flour • 120g Almonds, finely
ground • Finely grated zest of 2 lemons • Juice of
1 lemon • ¼ tsp Salt

Preheat the oven to 150°C/Gas Mark 2. Use baking parchment to line a 22 x 12cm loaf tin, 6cm deep, then butter it.

Roughly chop half the pine nuts. Beat the butter and sugar with the vanilla seeds until light and fluffy, then beat in the eggs one at a time. Fold in the flour, almonds and pine nuts, then stir in the lemon zest and juice.

Mix the remaining pine nuts with the salt. Spoon the mixture into the tin, scatter over the salted pine nuts and bake for 1 hour. The cake is ready when a skewer comes out clean. Cool in the tin.

31 Pistachio loaf cake

Serves 6-8

120g Pistachios, finely ground • 100g Blanched almonds, finely ground • 250g Unsalted butter, softened • 250g Caster sugar • 4 Eggs • Grated zest of 1 lemon • Seeds from 1 vanilla pod • 40g Plain flour

Topping
Juice and grated zest of 1 lemon • 50g Caster sugar • 60g Pistachios, halved

Preheat the oven to 150°C/Gas Mark 2. Line a 22 x 12cm x 6cm loaf tin with buttered baking parchment.

Beat the butter and sugar until light. Beat in the eggs one at a time. Add the lemon zest and vanilla seeds, fold in the pistachios and sift in the flour. Spoon the mixture into the tin and bake for 45 minutes. The cake is ready when a skewer comes out clean. Cool in the tin.

For the topping, mix the lemon juice with the sugar and boil until thick, then add the zest. Stir in the pistachios and pour the mixture over the cake.

32 Plum and orange cake

Serves 6

Plums
500g Ripe plums, halved and stoned • Juice and finely grated zest of 1 orange • 50g Caster sugar • 1 Vanilla pod, split lengthways

Cake
150g Unsalted butter, softened • 150g Caster sugar • 2 Eggs • 85g Self-raising flour • ½ tsp Baking powder • 100g Almonds, finely ground

Topping
30g Unsalted butter • 25g Muscovado sugar • Grated zest of 1 orange • 50g Flaked almonds

Preheat the oven to 180°C/Gas Mark 4. Line a 25cm cake tin with buttered baking parchment.

Put the plums in an ovenproof dish with the sugar, vanilla pod, orange juice and zest. Bake for 20 minutes. Cool. Scrape the vanilla seeds into the plums and discard the pod.

Beat the butter with the sugar until light. Beat in the eggs, one by one. Fold in the flour, baking powder and almonds. Pour into the tin and push the plums and their juices into the mixture. Bake for 30 minutes.

For the topping, melt the butter and stir in the sugar, orange zest and flaked almonds. Spread this over the half-baked cake, lower the heat to 160°C/Gas Mark 3 and bake for a further 20 minutes. Cool in the tin.

33 Orange almond whisky cake

Serves 6

Grated zest of 2 oranges • 300g Almonds, finely ground • Butter for greasing • 8 Eggs, separated • 200g Caster sugar • Grated zest of 2 lemons • Crème fraîche or mascarpone, to serve

Syrup
500ml Whisky • 320ml Freshly squeezed orange juice • 320ml Freshly squeezed lemon juice • 75g Caster sugar • 1 Cinnamon stick

Preheat the oven to 180°C/Gas Mark 4. Butter a 25cm square cake tin, 2cm deep, and line with baking parchment.

Beat the egg yolks with the sugar until pale, add the citrus zests and ground almonds and stir together briefly. Beat the egg whites to soft peaks and fold into the almond and egg yolk mixture. Pour into the cake tin and bake for 35-45 minutes, until set.

Make the syrup by heating the orange and lemon juice with the sugar and cinnamon in a pan over a moderate heat until reduced a little, then add the whisky.

When the cake is cooked and still hot, prick the whole surface with a sharp knife and pour over the syrup. Make sure all the liquid soaks into the cake. Remove the cake from the tin when completely cold. Serve with crème fraîche or mascarpone.

34 Vernazza loaf cake

Serves 6

250g Unsalted butter, softened • 225g Caster sugar •
4 Eggs • 3 Vanilla pods, split lengthways • 1 Egg yolk •
200g Plain flour • 1 tbs Potato flour • 1 tbs Polenta

Preheat the oven to 180°C/Gas Mark 4. Line the base
of a 22 × 12 × 6cm loaf tin with baking parchment.
Butter and flour generously.

Beat the butter and sugar together until pale and light,
then beat in the whole eggs, one at a time. Scrape the
vanilla seeds into the egg mixture, and add the
scraped pods and the egg yolk. Sift together the plain
flour and the potato flour and fold into the mixture.
Then fold in the polenta.

Pour the batter into the tin and bake for 45 minutes.
The cake is ready when a skewer comes out clean.

This simple loaf cake is delicious at the end of a meal
with a glass of Vin Santo or grappa, or at breakfast with
your cappucino.

Vernazza loaf cake (Recipe 34)

35 Almond, lemon, ricotta cake

Serves 8

250g Blanched almonds, coarsely chopped • Grated zest of 7 lemons • Juice of 3 lemons • 300g Ricotta • 225g Unsalted butter, softened • 65g Plain flour • 250g Caster sugar • 6 Eggs, separated

Preheat the oven to 150°C/Gas Mark 2.

Butter a 25cm round springform cake tin and line it with baking parchment. Combine the almonds with the flour and lemon zest. Using an electric mixer, beat the butter and sugar together until pale and light. Add the egg yolks, one by one, then the almond mixture.

Put the ricotta in a bowl and lightly beat with a fork. Add the lemon juice. In another bowl, beat the egg whites until they form soft peaks. Fold the egg whites into the almond mixture and finally stir in the ricotta.

Spoon the mixture into the tin and bake in the preheated oven for 35-40 minutes, until set. Test by inserting a skewer, which should come out clean. Remove from the tin while still warm and cool on a wire rack.

36 Lemon, ricotta, pine nut cake

Serves 6-8

Grated zest and juice of 3 lemons • 2 tbs Lemon essence • 600g Ricotta • 50g Pine nuts • 200g Caster sugar • 4 Eggs • 2 Egg yolks • 200ml Crème fraîche • 350g Mascarpone • 80g White breadcrumbs

Preheat the oven to 150°C/Gas Mark 2. Combine the lemon zest and juice and leave for 10 minutes.

Beat the ricotta and sugar until smooth. Add the eggs and egg yolks one at a time and continue beating. Add the crème fraîche. Fold in the lemon mixture, the mascarpone and the lemon essence.

Butter a 25cm round springform cake tin. Put the breadcrumbs in the tin and shake to coat all the sides evenly. Pour in the cake mixture, scatter over the pine nuts and bake for 45 minutes, until just set but not firm. Cool and turn out.

This is a Tuscan variation of the torta della Nonna, a traditional cake made at Easter with raisins and pastry.

Lemon, ricotta, pine nut cake (Recipe 36)

37 Hazelnut and ricotta cake

Serves 10

250g Shelled hazelnuts, roasted, skins rubbed off (see Recipe 12) and coarsely chopped • 250g Ricotta • 225g Unsalted butter, softened • 250g Caster sugar • 8 Eggs, separated • Finely grated zest of 5 lemons • 65g Plain flour • 150g 70% Chocolate, grated

Preheat the oven to 180°C/Gas Mark 4. Butter a 30cm round springform cake tin, 5cm deep, and line with baking parchment.

Using an electric mixer, beat the butter and sugar together until pale and light. Beat in the egg yolks one by one. In a large bowl, beat the ricotta lightly with a fork. Add the lemon zest and hazelnuts. In a separate bowl, beat the egg whites until they form soft peaks.

Fold the egg and butter mixture into the ricotta, then sift in the flour and finally fold in the beaten egg whites. Spoon into the prepared cake tin and bake for 35 minutes, until set.

Remove from the tin, leave for 5 minutes and, whilst still warm, cover with the chocolate, which will immediately melt.

38 Dada's Christmas cake

Serves 10

300g Blanched whole almonds • 250g Unsalted butter, softened • 350g Candied lemon and orange peel, coarsely chopped • 350ml Dark rum • 100g Caster sugar • 3 Eggs • 200g Plain flour • 100g Almonds, finely ground • Grated zest of 3 lemons • 150g Raisins • 200g Honey • 100g Apricot jam • 200g Shelled hazelnuts, roasted, skins rubbed off (see Recipe 12) • 500g 70% Chocolate, chopped

Preheat the oven to 160°C/Gas Mark 3.

Roast the blanched almonds in the oven for 5 minutes, then leave to cool. Chop coarsely.

Line a 23cm round cake tin with baking parchment and butter it. Marinate the candied lemon and orange peel in the rum for at least 1 hour.

Cream the butter and sugar together until pale and light. Beat in the eggs one at a time, then fold in the flour and ground almonds. Drain the fruit, reserving the rum, and add to the mixture, then add the lemon zest, raisins, honey and apricot jam. Fold in the roasted almonds and hazelnuts, the chocolate and the reserved rum. Pour into the prepared tin and bake at 150°C/Gas Mark 2 for 1 hour or until firm.

Dada's Christmas cake (Recipe 38)

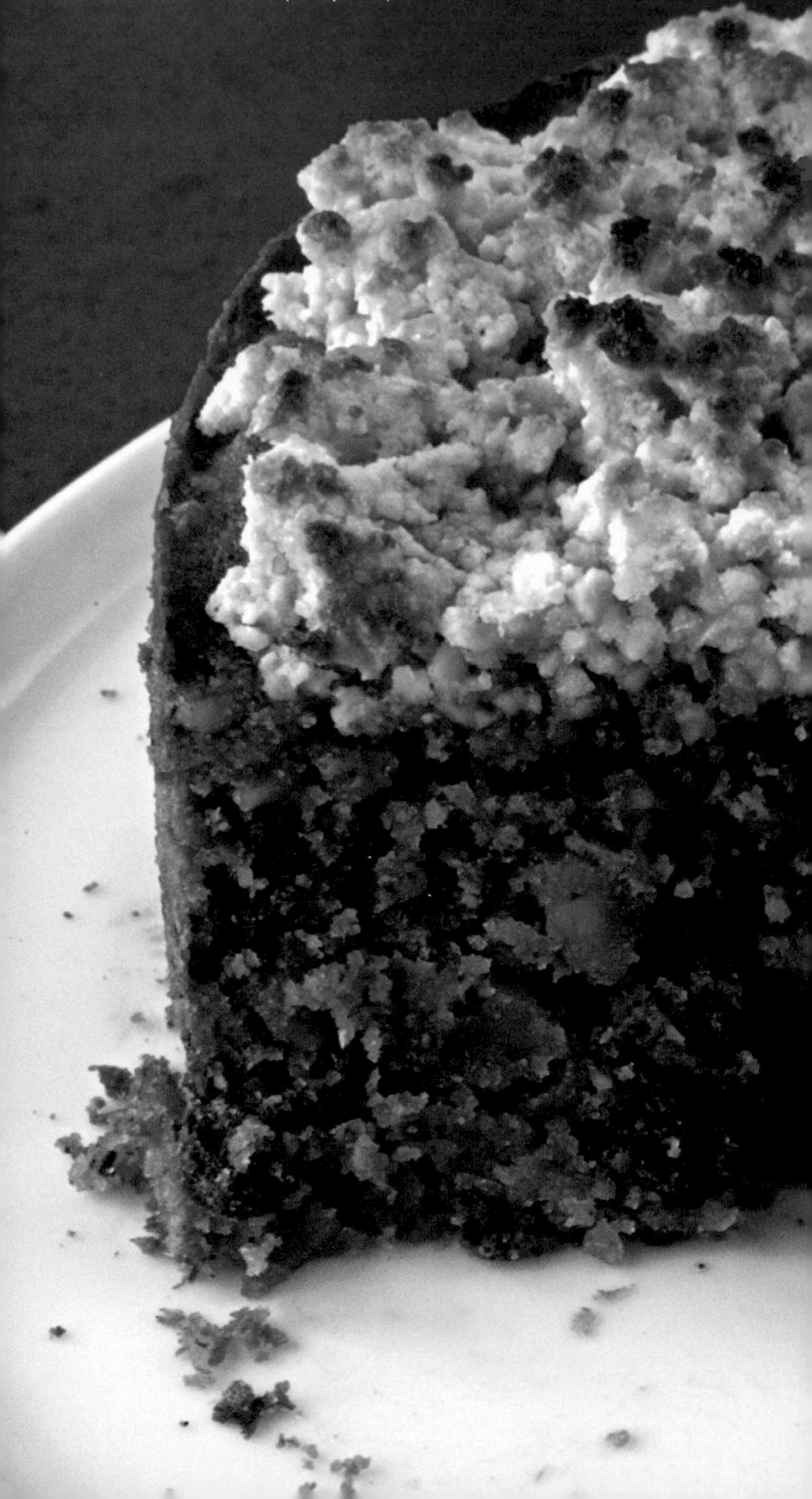

CHAPTER THREE
FRUIT

39 Summer fruit bruschetta

250g Blackcurrants • 2 Ripe peaches, halved and stoned • 4 Ripe plums, halved and stoned • 250g Raspberries • 250g Strawberries • 1 Vanilla pod, split lengthways • 100g Sugar • Juice of 1 lemon • 4 Slices of sourdough bread, cut 1.5cm thick, bottom crust removed • 50g Unsalted butter

Preheat the oven to 200°C/Gas Mark 6.

Put all the fruit into an oval baking dish with the vanilla pod. Sprinkle over the sugar and squeeze over the lemon juice . Bake for 20 minutes.

Grill the sourdough slices, then spread each one with butter. Spoon over the fruit and serve.

40 Plum and vanilla bruschetta

*500g Plums, halved and stoned • 2 Vanilla pods •
200g Caster sugar • 100g Unsalted butter • 4 Slices
of sourdough bread, cut 1cm thick, bottom crust
removed • 1 Lemon, cut into quarters • Crème fraîche,
to serve*

Preheat the oven to 180°C/Gas Mark 4.

Finely chop 1 vanilla pod and mix it with the caster
sugar. Split open the second vanilla pod lengthways.

Butter an ovenproof dish generously and put in the
plums, cut-side up. Scatter over half of the vanilla
sugar mix. Bake in the preheated oven for 15 minutes.

Butter the bread and scatter over the remaining
vanilla sugar mix. Place in the baking dish, piling the
half-cooked plums over. Squeeze over the juice from
the lemon quarters, then put the lemon quarters in
the dish. Continue to bake for 15 minutes. The bread
should be slightly crisp at the edges and soaked with
the plums and their juices in the middle. Serve with
crème fraîche.

41 Apricot bruschetta

4 Apricots, halved and stoned • 50g Unsalted butter,
softened • 4 Slices of sourdough bread, cut 1.5cm
thick, bottom crust removed • 2 Vanilla pods, cut into
small pieces • 250g Caster sugar • 4 Ripe nectarines,
halved and stoned • 4 Plums, halved and stoned •
50ml Brandy • Crème fraîche, to serve

Preheat the oven to 200°C/Gas Mark 6.

Butter a baking tray. Butter each slice of bread on one
side only. Roughly combine the vanilla with the sugar
in a food processor.

Put the fruits in a bowl. Stir in the vanilla sugar and the
brandy and leave to marinate for 20 minutes.

On each buttered slice of bread press 2 halves of
nectarine, cut-side down, so that they break up slightly
and the bread absorbs the juices. Place 2 halves of
apricot and plum, cut-side up, on top of each slice, and
pour over the remaining juices from the bowl.

Bake the bruschetta in the preheated oven for 25
minutes. They should be crisp on the edges and the
fruits cooked. Serve warm, with crème fraîche.

42   Baked nespole

1kg Nespole, halved and stoned • Seeds from 2 vanilla pods • 4 tbs Caster sugar • 120ml Brandy • Juice of 1 lemon • Crème fraîche, to serve

Preheat the oven to 160°C/Gas Mark 3.

Mix the vanilla seeds with the caster sugar. Place the nespole, cut-side up, in an ovenproof dish. Spoon a little of the vanilla sugar mixture on to each fruit. Sprinkle a few spoonfuls of brandy over, squeeze over the lemon juice, and bake for 45 minutes.

Serve with crème fraîche and a little more brandy over the fruit.

Nespola giapponese is the fruit known as the loquat, or Japanese medlar, which is native to China and Japan. Nespole ripen in the early spring. The skin is orange in colour, and there is a distinctive curved stone inside. When ripe, the white-to-yellow flesh is soft and pear like in texture, with a pleasant, acid-sweet flavour. The way we bake them is rather like making jam, which is how they are traditionally used.

43 Black figs baked with almonds

12 Black figs • 100g Blanched almonds, split • Juice of 1 lemon • 2 tbs Brown sugar • Crème fraîche, to serve

Preheat the oven to 150°C/Gas Mark 2.

Make a cross slash on the top of each fig, then squeeze from the bottom to open. Butter a shallow baking dish large enough to hold the figs. Place the figs in the dish and pour over the lemon juice. Sprinkle over the sugar and almonds.

Bake in the preheated oven for 10 minutes. Spoon over the juices and bake for a further 5 minutes. Serve warm, with crème fraîche.

44 Baked figs with crème fraîche

12 Ripe purple figs, stems removed, cut vertically in half • 250ml Crème fraîche • 120ml Grappa • 90ml Thick honey

Preheat the oven to 220°C/Gas Mark 7.

Put the figs in an ovenproof dish side by side, cut-side up. Wet the dish with 2 tbs of water. Place the figs in as close together as possible and drizzle a few drops of grappa over each. Spoon ½ tsp of honey over each fig and on top of that 1 tsp of crème fraîche.

Place the dish high up in the oven for 5 minutes, or until the cream is slightly brown and the juices are running from the figs. Serve immediately.

45   Baked apples with walnuts

4 Bramley apples • 100g Shelled walnuts • 2 Oranges • 200g Caster sugar • 50g Unsalted butter • Crème fraîche, to serve

Grate the zest of 1 orange and squeeze the juice. Cut up the second orange, and pound it in a mortar. Push this through a sieve and reserve the bitter pulp.

Put the sugar in a small saucepan with enough water just to cover. Gently melt the sugar into a syrup, then add the zest and pulp of the oranges. Turn up the heat and boil to a light caramel.

Wet a small oval dish with a spray of water. Place the walnuts in it and pour the caramel over them. Leave to cool and set hard. Turn out and crack up the caramel into 2-3cm pieces.

Preheat the oven to 160°C/Gas Mark 3.

Core the apples and peel around the top 1/3 of each one. Stuff the caramel and a little butter into the holes.

Butter an ovenproof dish and put in the apples. Scatter any spare caramel pieces around. Pour in the orange juice, lightly cover with foil and bake in the preheated oven for 45 minutes. Serve with crème fraîche.

Baked apples with walnuts (Recipe 45)

46 Baked apricots with molasses

*600g Apricots, halved and stoned • 100g Molasses •
50g Fresh root ginger, peeled and finely sliced • 50g
Unsalted butter • Juice of 1 lemon • Crème fraîche, to
serve*

Preheat the oven to 180°C/Gas Mark 4.

Butter a flat ovenproof dish. Place the apricots in the
dish, cut-side up. Place a few pieces of ginger on each
apricot, with a small knob of butter and 1 tsp
molasses. Sprinkle with the lemon juice.

Place in the preheated oven and bake for 30 minutes.
Serve with crème fraîche.

47 Baked pears with Marsala

*4 Ripe Comice pears • 175ml Marsala • 50g
Unsalted butter, at room temperature • 100g Soft dark
brown sugar • 50ml White wine • 2 Cinnamon sticks,
roughly broken • Crème fraîche, to serve*

Preheat the oven to 180°C/Gas Mark 4.

Cut a thin slice off the base of each pear, so that it will
stand up, then hollow out the core from the bottom.
Spread a little butter over the skin of each pear and
stand them in an ovenproof dish. Dust with the sugar.
Pour the Marsala and white wine into the dish. Scatter
the cinnamon sticks over the pears, then cover the
dish loosely with foil.

Bake for about 30 minutes, remove the foil and lower the oven temperature to 150°C/Gas Mark 2. Continue to bake for 30 minutes, until the pears are very tender and slightly shrivelled. Serve warm, with their juices and some crème fraîche.

48 Baked pears with Valpolicella

4 Comice pears • Pared zest of 1 lemon, in long strips, plus the juice • 2 tbs Caster sugar • 1 Vanilla pod, split lengthways • 2 tbs Soft brown sugar • Crème fraîche, to serve

Caramel
150ml Valpolicella • 300g Caster sugar • 120ml Water

Preheat the oven to 180°C/Gas Mark 4.

Cut a thin slice off the base of each pear, so that it will stand up, then hollow out the core from the bottom. Put a piece of lemon zest, ½ tbs of caster sugar and some of the vanilla seeds inside each pear. Put the pears upright in a baking dish. Sprinkle with the lemon juice, cover with foil and bake for 10 minutes, until the juice has been absorbed. Remove the foil.

For the caramel, heat the sugar and water together gently, then boil until it forms a dark caramel. Carefully add the Valpolicella. Pour the caramel over the pears and bake for 40 minutes, basting every 10 minutes, until the pears are shrivelled.

Remove from the oven and sprinkle with the brown sugar. Serve with crème fraîche.

Baked pears with Valpolicella (Recipe 48)

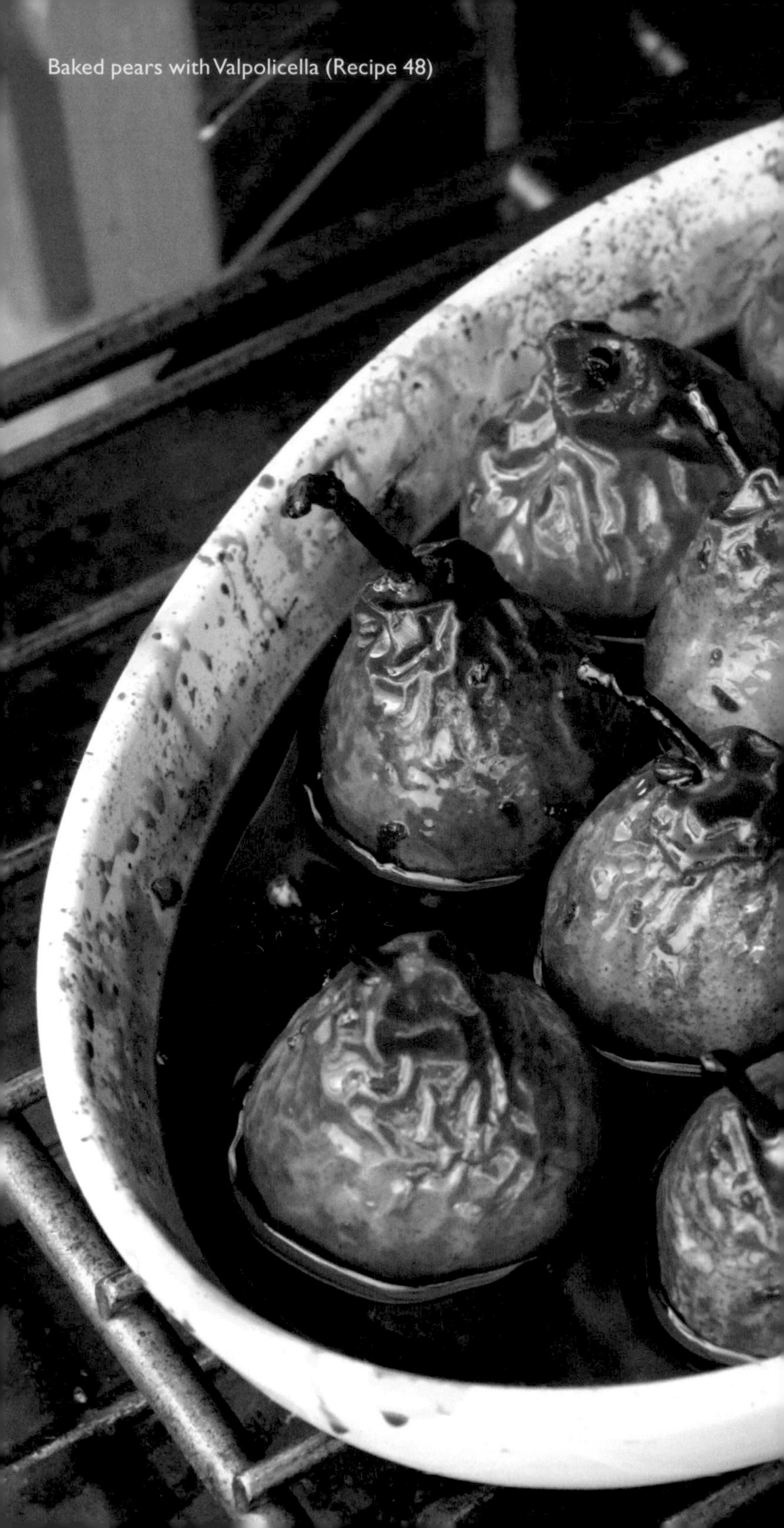

49 Baked whole pear with cinnamon and grappa

4 Ripe Comice pears • 2 Cinnamon sticks, broken in half • 200ml Grappa • 100g Unsalted butter, softened • 2 tbs Soft brown sugar • 2 Vanilla pods, split lengthways • Crème fraîche, to serve

Preheat the oven to 150°C/Gas Mark 2.

Cut a small slice from the bottom of each pear so that they will stand in the dish. Butter a baking dish large enough to hold the pears. Rub some butter over each pear, place in the dish and sprinkle over the sugar, vanilla and cinnamon sticks. Cover the dish with foil.

Bake in the preheated oven for 20 minutes, then remove the foil and add the grappa. Return to the oven and bake for a further 20 minutes or until the pears are very tender.

Serve warm, with the juices and some crème fraîche.

50 Baked rhubarb with orange

500g Champagne rhubarb, cut into 5cm lengths • 1 Blood orange • 2 Vanilla pods, split lengthways • 3 tbs Demerara sugar • Crème fraîche, to serve

Preheat the oven to 150°C/Gas Mark 2.

Finely grate the zest of half the orange, then squeeze the juice. Scrape out vanilla seeds from the pods.

Lay the rhubarb pieces in a small baking dish. Scatter over the vanilla seeds, sugar and orange zest. Add the vanilla pods. Pour over the orange juice and bake in the preheated oven for 15-20 minutes.

Serve with crème fraîche.

51 Baked quince with brown sugar

2 Quinces • 150g Soft brown sugar • 100g Unsalted butter • 1 Lemon • Crème fraîche, to serve

Preheat the oven to 160°C/Gas Mark 3.

Brush the down from the quinces, cut them in half and cut out the cores.

Thickly butter an ovenproof dish. Scatter the sugar over it, reserving 4 tsp. Put a knob of butter and 1 tsp of sugar in the core cavity of each quince half and place the quinces in the dish, cut-side down. Squeeze over a little lemon juice, then bake in the preheated oven for 30 minutes, or until soft.

Serve with the juices and some crème fraîche.

52 Peaches in Moscadello

6 White peaches • 1 Bottle of Moscadello • 50g Caster sugar • 3 Vanilla pods, split lengthways

Simmer the wine, sugar and vanilla pods for 5 minutes, stirring to dissolve the sugar.

Add the peaches to the liquid, bring back to simmering point, then lower the heat and cook gently for 3 minutes. Remove the pan from the heat, leave the peaches to cool, then peel them, cut them in half and remove the stones.

Put the peaches in a bowl and pour over the liquid and vanilla pods. Serve at room temperature.

53 Peaches in Pinot Nero

6 White peaches, halved and stoned • 1 Bottle of Pinot Nero • Pared zest of 2 lemons • 6 tbs Caster sugar

Cut the lemon zest into pieces, making sure you remove any bitter white pith.

Cut the peach halves into slices 3mm thick. Put in a deep bowl, sprinkle with the sugar, cover with the wine and add the lemon zest. Cover with cling film and leave to marinate for an hour in a cool place. Serve in wine glasses.

54 Raspberries with fresh ricotta

4 Punnets of raspberries • 250g Ricotta • Finely grated zest of 1 lemon • 4 tbs Caster sugar

Mix the lemon zest with the sugar. Leave to allow the flavours to combine and the sugar to be absorbed.

Scatter the raspberries over a large plate. Very carefully turn the ricotta out of the tub and then slice it as finely as possible. Place these ricotta slices carefully over the raspberries. Sprinkle with the lemon sugar.

55 Melon in Soave Classico

Serves 8

*4 Large, ripe Cavaillon melons, or 6 small ones •
1 Bottle of Soave Classico • Juice of 1 lemon*

Cool the Soave Classico in the fridge for 1 hour.

Cut the melons in half and scoop out the seeds. Scrape out the flesh in big pieces and place into individual glasses. Pour lemon juice over each serving and fill each glass with the Soave. Leave in the fridge for 1 hour.

Melon in Soave Classico (Recipe 55)

56 Wild strawberries

Wild strawberries • Lemon • Sugar

We have not given amounts of lemon and sugar, as it depends on how many wild strawberries you have. Allow a punnet per person, and 1/2 lemon and 1 tbs of sugar per punnet.

Squeeze the lemon juice and stir with the sugar until dissolved. Pour over the wild strawberries and marinate for 30 minutes, gently turning the fruits over in the juice a few times.

Serve with caster sugar sprinkled over the top.

In restaurants in Italy you often see an array of glass bowls of these wild strawberries, which have been marinated with sugar and lemon.

57 Grilled peaches with Amaretto

4 Peaches, halved and stoned • 120ml Amaretto liqueur • 1 Vanilla pod, split open lengthways • 2 tbs Caster sugar • Crème fraîche, to serve

Preheat the oven to 190°C/Gas Mark 5.

Preheat a chargrill or griddle pan. Put the vanilla pod into a mortar with the sugar. Pound with the pestle until broken up and combined.

Arrange the peach halves cut-side up. Scatter with half the vanilla sugar.

Carefully, place the peach halves cut-side down onto the chargrill pan and grill very briefly just to colour. Pour over the Amaretto and serve hot or cold, with the remaining sugar and the crème fraîche.

Amaretto, known as Disaronno, is an Italian liqueur flavoured with herbs and fruits soaked in apricot kernel oil.

58 Almond meringue with strawberries and cream

Serves 14

Meringue
175g Almonds, finely ground • Olive oil and butter for greasing • 5 Egg whites • 225g Caster sugar • 110g Unsalted butter, melted • 70g Plain flour

Strawberries and cream
1.5kg Strawberries, hulled and halved • 1 litre Double cream • Seeds from 1 vanilla pod • 150g Icing sugar • 150ml Brandy

Preheat the oven to 120°C/Gas Mark ½. Rub olive oil over 3 flat baking trays. Line each tray with baking parchment and generously butter the paper.

Using an electric mixer, beat the egg whites with half the sugar until stiff, then add the almonds and the remaining sugar. Beat briefly just to combine. Fold in the melted butter. Sift in the flour and fold in carefully.

Spoon the mixture onto the 3 trays and spread it out flat, each the same shape and diameter, as thinly as you can (1cm thick at most). Bake for 50 minutes, or until set and nearly crisp. Immediately peel off the paper whilst the meringues are still hot. Cool on wire racks.

Lightly whip the cream with the vanilla seeds and icing sugar. When stiff, fold in the brandy.

Place the first meringue on a large, flat serving plate and cover it with ⅓ of the cream. Place ⅓ of the strawberries on top of the cream. Repeat twice more.

59 Summer pudding with Valpolicella

Serves 8

*½ Bottle of Valpolicella Classico • 150g Caster sugar •
350g Blackcurrants (or small strawberries), stalks and
leaves removed • 350g Redcurrants, stalks and leaves
removed • 350g Raspberries (or blackberries) •
2 Vanilla pods, split lengthways • Juice of ½ lemon •
½ Sourdough loaf, crusts removed, cut into slices 1cm
thick • Crème fraîche, to serve*

Dissolve the sugar in 50ml water in a thick-bottomed
pan, then boil until the syrup begins to colour to a
light caramel. Remove from the heat, carefully add the
Valpolicella and stir.

Add ⅔ of each type of fruit, plus the vanilla pods, to
the hot syrup, and return to the stove. Heat gently,
stirring, until the fruits begin to release their juices. Try
not to break up the fruit. Remove from the heat and
add the lemon juice and the uncooked fruit.

Line a 20cm bowl with the bread, so that there are no
gaps. Keep aside enough slices to cover the top. Pour
the fruit mixture into the bowl; it should easily come
to the top, the juices soaking into the bread. Cover
with a layer of bread slices, pushing them into the fruit
to soak up the juice. Weight down with a small plate
that just fits into the bowl, then put a weight on top of
that. Put in the fridge for at least 4 hours.

Turn out and serve with crème fraîche.

Summer pudding with Valpolicella (Recipe 56)

CHAPTER FOUR

CREAM DESSERTS

60 Panna cotta

Serves 6

*1 litre Double cream • 2 Vanilla pods, split lengthways •
2 1/2 Gelatine leaves • 125ml Milk • 125g Icing sugar*

Heat 750ml of the cream in a thick-bottomed pan.
Add the vanilla, bring to the boil and simmer until
reduced by one third. Remove the pods and scrape
the seeds into the cream.

Soak the gelatine in the milk for 15 minutes. Remove
the gelatine, then heat the milk until boiling. Remove
from the heat, return the gelatine to the milk and stir
until dissolved. Add to the hot cream and cool.

Whip the remaining cream with the icing sugar. Fold it
into the cooled cooked cream. Pour into six 200ml
bowls and leave in the fridge to set for 2 hours.

61 Panna cotta with raspberries

Serves 6

*Panna cotta (see Recipe 60) • 3 Punnets of
raspberries • 120ml Grappa, plus extra to serve*

Follow the panna cotta recipe, adding the grappa to
the cooled cooked cream before pouring it into
bowls.

Turn out the set creams onto plates and serve with
the raspberries and 1 tbs of extra grappa poured
over the top.

62 Panna cotta with chocolate

Serves 6

Panna cotta (see Recipe 60) • 300g 70% Chocolate, broken into small pieces • 45g Unsalted butter

Melt the chocolate and the butter in a bowl set over a pan of simmering water. Do not let the water touch the bowl.

Turn out the set creams onto plates, pour over the chocolate and serve immediately. This has to be done at the last minute or the chocolate will stiffen.

63 Panna cotta with caramel

Serves 6

Panna cotta (see Recipe 60) • 250g Caster sugar • 4-6 Strips of thinly pared orange zest • 5cm Piece of cinnamon stick • 120ml Freshly squeezed orange juice • Brandy, to serve

Place the sugar, 175ml of water, orange zest and cinnamon in a thick-bottomed saucepan. Slowly bring to the boil to melt the sugar, then boil until reduced to a thick, dark caramel. Cool, remove the cinnamon, then stir in the orange juice. Wet six 200ml bowls and spoon 2 tbs of the caramel into each.

Follow the panna cotta recipe to the point of adding the cream. Pour onto the caramel, cool for 2 hours. Turn out the set creams and pour over the brandy.

64 Panna cotta with rhubarb

Panna cotta (see Recipe 60) • 500g Champagne rhubarb, cut into 5-6cm lengths • 1 Blood orange • 2 Vanilla pods • 3 tbs Demerara sugar

Preheat the oven to 150°C/Gas Mark 2.

Finely grate the zest of half the orange, then squeeze the juice. Split the vanilla pods open lengthways and scrape out the seeds.

Lay the rhubarb pieces in a small baking dish. Scatter over the vanilla seeds, sugar and orange zest. Add the vanilla pods. Pour over the orange juice and bake in the preheated oven for 15-20 minutes.

Serve with the panna cotta.

65 Mascarpone cream

500g Mascarpone • 3 Egg yolks • 120g Icing sugar

Beat the mascarpone lightly. In a separate bowl, beat the egg yolks. Add the icing sugar to the egg yolks, then fold in the mascarpone. Keep cool until you serve. This is delicious served with fruit or biscuits.

66 Blackberries with mascarpone

*1kg Blackberries • 500g Mascarpone • 3 Egg yolks •
Seeds from 2 vanilla pods • 30g Icing sugar*

Preheat the oven to 200°C/Gas Mark 6.

Pick over the blackberries and put them in a baking
dish. Mix the mascarpone, egg yolks, vanilla seeds and
sugar together. Spoon the mixture over the
blackberries and bake in the preheated oven until the
mascarpone begins to brown, about 5 minutes.

67 Sweet ricotta

*400g Ricotta, drained of any liquid • 3 tbs Icing
sugar • 2 tbs Dark rum • 2 tsp Finely ground espresso
coffee beans*

Beat the ricotta with a fork to lighten it, then add the
sugar, rum and coffee. Mix well. Put in the fridge to
chill. This can be served with tart fruit, such as Baked
Nespole (see Recipe 42).

68 Monte Bianco

500g Fresh chestnuts • 1 litre Milk • 100g Caster sugar • 2 Vanilla pods, split lengthways and seeds loosened • 250ml Crème fraîche • A little good-quality bitter chocolate

Bring a large saucepan of water to the boil. Score the chestnuts across the round sides of their outer shells. Drop them into the boiling water and boil for 15-20 minutes. Remove a few chestnuts from the water at a time; the shell will come off easily, so long as the chestnuts are kept hot in the cooking water. Squeeze each chestnut to crack open the shell, then prise the nuts out of the shell. Remove the bitter inner skin.

Heat the milk in a large pan, add the sugar, split vanilla pods and chestnuts, and simmer gently for 40 minutes, until the chestnuts become quite soft. Put the cooked chestnuts through a coarse mouli. Add enough of the remaining reduced milk to bring the mixture together into a thick dough. Taste for sweetness.

Using a small plain nozzle, pipe the chestnut dough out into a mountain shape on a flat serving platter; this will take some time! Serve with the crème fraîche, with some bitter chocolate grated on top.

This is a wonderful winter dessert. A mountain of puréed sweet chestnuts, covered with crème fraîche and a scattering of bitter chocolate. Named after Monte Bianco in the Italian Alps, the cream should fall down the slopes of chestnut, resembling the snow.

69 Tiramisu

8 tbs Instant coffee • 300ml Brandy • 250g Savoiardi biscuits • 2 Eggs, separated • 75g Icing sugar • 500g Mascarpone • 25g Cocoa powder

Dissolve the instant coffee in 225ml hot water. Mix the coffee with the brandy. Lay the biscuits out on a flat tray and soak them in the coffee and brandy.

Mix the egg yolks and icing sugar into the mascarpone. Beat the egg whites until they form soft peaks, then fold them into the mascarpone.

In an oval 35 x 24cm ceramic dish, make a layer of wet biscuits. Cover with a thick layer of mascarpone. Shake over some cocoa powder, then repeat with a further layer of biscuits and mascarpone. Shake over cocoa powder, then chill for a minimum of 2 hours before serving.

There are endless variations on this modern dessert. Ours is very rich and wet with lots of alcohol and mascarpone.

CHAPTER
FIVE
ICE CREAMS

---

70 Vanilla ice cream

Serves 10

4 Vanilla pods, split lengthways • 1.5 litres Double cream • 450ml Milk • 20 Egg yolks • 350g Caster sugar

In a large, heavy saucepan combine the cream and milk. Scrape the vanilla seeds out of the pods into the pan, then add the pods. Heat to just below boiling.

Beat the egg yolks and sugar slowly for 10 minutes until pale and thick. Pour a little of the warm cream onto the egg yolks and combine. Return to the saucepan and cook gently over a low heat, stirring constantly to prevent the mixture curdling. When it has thickened and is almost boiling, strain into a bowl and let cool.

Put in an ice-cream machine and churn until frozen, or freeze in a shallow container, stirring every half hour.

---

71 Roasted almond ice cream

Serves 10

4 Vanilla pods, split lengthways • 1.5 litres Double cream • 450ml Milk • 20 Egg yolks • 350g Caster sugar

Roast almonds
250g Blanched almonds • 15g Unsalted butter • 2 tbs Caster sugar

Follow the instructions for making vanilla ice cream (see Recipe 70), until the mixture is strained and left to cool.

Preheat the oven to 180°C/Gas Mark 4.

Place the almonds on a flat baking tray and roast until lightly browned. Add the butter and sugar, mix and roast for a further 10 minutes. Cool.

Put the almonds on one half of a kitchen cloth, fold the other half over and bash into bits with a rolling pin. Stir the almonds into the vanilla ice cream mixture.

Put in an ice-cream machine and churn until frozen, or freeze in a shallow container, stirring every half hour.

72 Stracciatella ice cream

Serves 10

4 Vanilla pods, split lengthways • 1.5 litres Double cream • 450ml Milk • 15 Egg yolks • 350g Caster sugar • 350g 70% Chocolate, chopped

Follow the instructions for making vanilla ice cream (see Recipe 70), until the mixture is strained and left to cool.

When cool, fold in the chocolate. Put in an ice-cream machine and churn until frozen, or freeze in a shallow container, stirring every half hour.

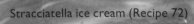
Stracciatella ice cream (Recipe 72)

73 Vanilla risotto ice cream

Serves 10

*4 Vanilla pods, split lengthways • 450ml Milk •
1.75 litres Double cream • 15 Egg yolks • 350g
Caster sugar*

Risotto
*3 Vanilla pods, split lengthways • 2 litres Milk • 500g
Vialone nano rice • 100g Vanilla sugar (see Recipe 40)
• ½ Nutmeg, freshly grated • Grated zest of 2 lemons*

Follow the instructions for making vanilla ice cream
(see Recipe 70), until the mixture is strained and left
to cool.

For the risotto, scrape the seeds from the vanilla
pods. Heat the milk in a large saucepan and add the
vanilla seeds and pods. Bring to the boil, then add the
rice, sugar, nutmeg and lemon zest. Lower the heat
and simmer, stirring, until the rice is soft and the milk
has been absorbed, about 45 minutes. Remove the
pods, pour the mixture into a bowl and cool.

Place the rice mixture in a food processor and pulse-
chop to a coarse purée. Combine this with the
custard. Put in an ice-cream machine and churn until
frozen, or freeze in a shallow container, stirring every
half hour or so.

74 Chocolate whisky ice cream

Serves 10

450g 70% Chocolate, broken into small pieces • 200ml Whisky • 1.75 litres Double cream • 450ml Milk • 4 Vanilla pods, split lengthways • 15 Egg yolks • 350g Caster sugar

Follow the instructions for making vanilla ice cream (see Recipe 70), until the mixture is strained into a bowl. Whilst still warm, add the chocolate and stir until it has melted. Leave to cool, then add the whisky.

Put in an ice-cream machine and churn until frozen, or freeze in a shallow container, stirring every half hour.

75 Caramel ice cream

1.75 litres Double cream • 450ml Milk • 4 Vanilla pods, split lengthways • 20 Egg yolks • 350g Caster sugar

Caramel
275g Caster sugar

Follow the instructions for vanilla ice cream (see Recipe 70), until the mixture is strained and cooled.

To make the caramel, dissolve the sugar in 120ml of water in a thick-bottomed pan, then boil until almost black and smoking. Carefully add this to the custard and stir. Leave to cool.

Put in an ice-cream machine and churn until frozen, or freeze in a shallow container, stirring every half hour.

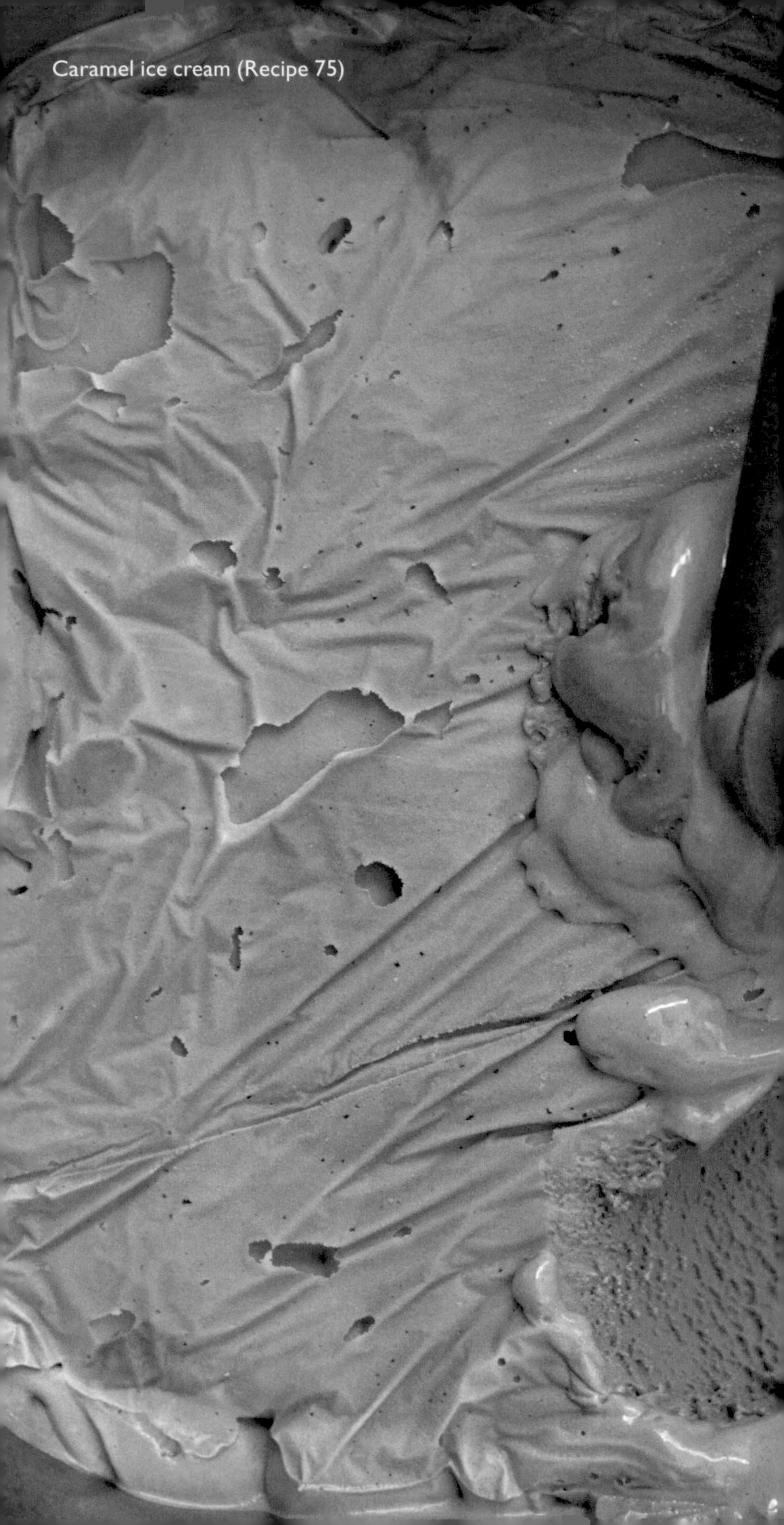

Caramel ice cream (Recipe 75)

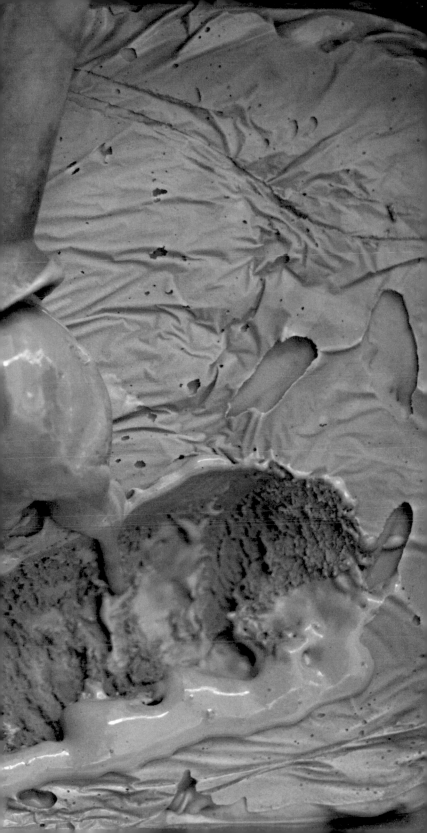

76   Hazelnut ice cream

1.75 litres Double cream • 450ml Milk • 15 Egg yolks • 350g Caster sugar

Praline
500g Shelled hazelnuts, roasted, skins rubbed off (see Recipe 12) • 450g Caster sugar

Follow the instructions for making vanilla ice cream (see Recipe 70), omitting the vanilla pods, until the mixture is strained.

To make the caramel for the praline, gently heat the sugar and 300ml water in a heavy saucepan until the sugar has dissolved, then bring to the boil and boil until almost smoking. Pour the caramel over the hazelnuts in a baking tin and leave to cool until solid. Break up the praline and blend in a food processor until as fine as possible. Add to the ice cream mixture and stir well.

Pour the ice cream mixture through a fine chinois sieve. Put the bits of praline left in the chinois in a saucepan and cook until dark brown, about 5-6 minutes. Return to the chinois and press through, then stir into the ice cream. Put in an ice-cream machine and churn until frozen, or freeze in a shallow container, stirring every half hour or so.

77 Hazelnut praline semifreddo

*650ml Double cream • 900ml Milk • 8 Egg yolks •
175g Caster sugar • 120ml Frangelico*

Praline
*300g Shelled hazelnuts, roasted and skins rubbed off
(see Recipe 12) • 225g Caster sugar*

For the praline, heat the sugar and 150ml water in a
saucepan until the sugar has dissolved, then bring to
the boil and cook until it turns to a dark caramel.
Place the nuts in a baking tin and pour over the
caramel. Let cool. Finely chop the praline finely in a
food processor.

Combine 300ml of the cream with the milk and heat
to just below boiling. Remove from the heat. Whisk
the egg yolks with the sugar until pale. Mix a cup of
the hot cream mixture into the egg yolks, then
transfer the mixture back to the pan. Cook over a low
heat, stirring, until the mixture has thickened enough
to coat the back of a spoon. Pour into a bowl. Cool.

Stir the praline powder into the custard, then pour
through a sieve into a bowl. Put the praline remaining
in the sieve back into the pan with a ladleful of
custard and cook, stirring, for a few minutes. Strain
back into the custard. Put into an ice-cream machine
and churn until softly frozen.

Lightly beat the remaining double cream and fold in
the Frangelico. Mix into the semifreddo and return to
the freezer.

78 Tartufo

600ml Milk • 4 Egg yolks • 100g Caster sugar • 220g 100% Chocolate, broken into small pieces • 220g 70% Chocolate, broken into pieces • 5 tbs Double cream

In a thick-bottomed saucepan, heat the milk to just below boiling point. Whisk the egg yolks with the sugar until thick, then add the hot milk, whisking all the time. Return to the pan and cook over a low heat, stirring, until the mixture thickens enough to coat the back of the spoon. Remove from the heat.

Melt the 100% chocolate with half the 70% chocolate in a bowl over a pan of simmering water. The water should not touch the bowl. Remove from the heat and slowly add the hot custard, whisking. Cool.

Stir in the cream. Put in an ice-cream machine and churn until frozen, or freeze in a shallow container, stirring every half hour or so. About 5 minutes before it is frozen, mix in the remaining pieces of 70% chocolate and continue to churn or freeze until set.

79 Espresso ice cream

225g Good-quality instant coffee • 1.75 litres Double cream • 450ml Milk • 4 Vanilla pods, split lengthways • 20 Egg yolks • 350g Caster sugar

Follow the instructions for making vanilla ice cream (see Recipe 70), until the mixture has thickened.

Put the instant coffee into a bowl and add 30ml of the hot custard. Stir until the granules have dissolved. Return this mixture to the saucepan and stir well; it should be a very dark colour. Allow to cool.

Put in an ice-cream machine and churn until frozen, or freeze in a shallow container, stirring every half hour.

80 Vin Santo ice cream

¾ Bottle of Vin Santo • 20 Egg yolks • 400g Caster sugar • 1 litre Double cream

Beat the egg yolks and sugar together until they have trebled in volume. Transfer to a large bowl set over a pan of simmering water. The water must not touch the bowl. Cook, stirring constantly, until the mixture comes just to the boil – about 20 minutes. Leave to cool.

Slightly whip the double cream and stir in the cooled custard, along with the Vin Santo. Put in an ice-cream machine and churn until frozen, or freeze in a shallow container, stirring every half hour.

81 Marsala ice cream

350ml Dry Marsala • 10 Egg yolks • 200g Caster sugar • 450ml Double cream

Beat the egg yolks and the sugar until they have trebled in volume. Transfer to a large bowl and set over a pan of simmering water. The water should not touch the bowl. Cook, stirring constantly until the mixture comes just to the boil – about 20 minutes. Leave to cool.

If using an ice-cream machine, just add the cream and churn. If not, beat the cream before folding it into the mixture, then freeze in a shallow container, stirring every half hour.

82 Zabaglione ice cream

20 Egg yolks • 400g Caster sugar • 120ml Bristol Cream sherry • 85ml Dark rum • 1 litre Double cream

Place the egg yolks and sugar in an electric mixer and beat until light and fluffy, at least 10 minutes. Add half of the sherry and rum, then transfer the mixture to a bowl that will fit over a large saucepan of boiling water. The water should not touch the bowl. Whisk continuously until the mixture comes almost to the boil – this will take at least 20 minutes.

Stir in the remaining sherry and rum and leave to cool. If you are using an ice-cream machine, add the cream and churn. If freezing directly in the freezer, beat the cream to soft peaks, fold it into the mixture, then freeze in a suitable container.

83 Lemon ice cream

Serves 6

Juice and finely grated zest of 3 lemons • 200g Caster sugar • 450ml Double cream • ½ tsp Salt

Combine the lemon juice and zest with the sugar. Slowly add the cream and salt, mixing carefully. It will immediately thicken. Freeze in a shallow container.

84 Lemon and ricotta ice cream

Juice and finely grated zest of 7 lemons • 500g Ricotta, roughly crumbled • 1.75 litres Double cream • 450ml Milk • 20 Egg yolks • 350g Caster sugar

Follow the instructions for making vanilla ice cream (see Recipe 70), omitting the vanilla, until the mixture is strained into a bowl.

Add the lemon juice and zest and the ricotta to the cream mixture and stir briefly. Put in an ice-cream machine and churn until frozen, or freeze in a shallow container, stirring every half hour.

85 Mascarpone ice cream

2.25kg Mascarpone • Juice of 3 lemons • 400g Caster sugar • 350ml Water • 20 Egg yolks

Heat the sugar and water gently in a thick-bottomed saucepan until the sugar has dissolved. Add the lemon juice and boil until a syrup has formed.

In a bowl, beat the egg yolks until pale and light, then add the syrup in a trickle, whisking all the time. Place the bowl over a pan of simmering water – the water must not touch the bowl – and whisk continuously until the mixture is thick. Remove from the heat and whisk until cool. Whisk in the mascarpone.

Put in an ice-cream machine and churn until frozen, or freeze in a shallow container, stirring every half hour.

86 Lemon semifreddo

Grated zest and juice of 4 lemons • 4 Eggs, separated • 200g Caster sugar • 250ml Double cream • 1 tsp Fine salt

Mix the lemon zest and juice together.

Beat the egg yolks with the sugar in an electric mixer until light, at least 8 minutes. Place the mixture in a bowl set over a large saucepan of simmering water (do not let the water touch the bowl). Whisk continuously until the mixture is very hot, but not quite boiling or the eggs will scramble. Cool, then add the lemon mixture. Lightly beat the cream and fold it in. In a separate bowl, beat the egg whites with the salt until stiff. Fold into the lemon and egg yolk mixture.

Use baking parchment to line a tin that will fit in the freezer. Pour in the mixture and freeze until firm.

87 Blackcurrant ice cream

I kg Blackcurrants, stalks and leaves removed • 300g Caster sugar • Juice of I lemon • 500ml Double cream

Put the blackcurrants into a suitably large saucepan. Add the sugar and heat gently, stirring to break up the fruit. As soon as the juices begin to flow and the blackcurrants change colour to a deep red, remove from the heat. Allow to cool, then push the fruit juice and pulp through a fine sieve. Add the lemon juice.

In a separate bowl, very lightly whip the cream to thicken it slightly. Fold one serving spoon of cream into the fruit purée, then quickly mix the fruit purée into the cream. Stir gently to combine. Put in an ice-cream machine and churn until frozen, or freeze in a shallow container, stirring every half hour or so.

88 Fig ice cream

Serves 10

8 Black figs • 3 tbs Dark brown sugar • Juice of ½ lemon • 1.5 litres Double cream • 450ml Milk • 4 Vanilla pods, split lengthways • 20 Egg yolks • 350g Caster sugar

Put the figs in a bowl and pour over boiling water, just to colour the skin. Remove from the water and dry. Cut off the stalks and chop the figs roughly. Add the sugar and lemon juice. Stir to mix.

Follow the instructions for making vanilla ice cream (see Recipe 70), until the mixture is cool.

Stir the fig mixture into the custard. Put in an ice-cream machine and churn until frozen, or freeze in a shallow container, stirring every half hour or so.

89 Plum ice cream

2kg Dark-skinned plums • 1.75 litres Double cream • 450ml Milk • 2 Vanilla pods, split lengthways • 20 Egg yolks • 500g Caster sugar

Follow the instructions for making vanilla ice cream (see Recipe 70), using 350g of the sugar, until the mixture is cool.

Put the plums into a large saucepan with a tight-fitting lid. Add the remaining sugar, cover and gently heat to boiling point. Remove and allow to cool. Push the fruit and juices through a sieve.

Stir the custard into the plum purée, a ladleful at a time. Test for sweetness, and remember that ice cream should taste sweeter before freezing. According to the type of plum, you may not need to add all the vanilla custard.

Put in an ice-cream machine and churn until frozen, or freeze in a shallow container, stirring every half hour.

90 Peach ice cream

Serves 10

2kg Ripe white peaches, peeled, halved and stoned • 4 Vanilla pods, split lengthways • 1.75 litres Double cream • 450ml Milk • 15 Egg yolks • 350g Caster sugar, plus 1 tbs • Juice of 1 lemon

Follow the instructions for making vanilla ice cream (see Recipe 70), until the mixture is cool.

Smash the peaches into a thick purée with a fork and sprinkle with 1 tbs sugar and the lemon juice. Stir the peaches into the cream. Put in an ice-cream machine and churn until frozen, or freeze in a shallow container, stirring every half hour.

Peach ice cream (Recipe 90)

91 Orange ice cream

Juice and finely grated zest of 8 oranges • Juice and finely grated zest of I lemon • 200g Caster sugar • 500ml Double cream • 4 tbs Grand Marnier

Put the grated zests into a bowl. Add the juice of 2 oranges and leave to steep. Put the remaining orange juice in a pan with the sugar and bring to the boil. Boil until it becomes a thick syrup. Cool.

Whip the cream to soft peaks. Stir the reserved juice and zest into the syrup and add the lemon juice. Stir this mixture into the cream. It will immediately thicken. Add the Grand Marnier.

Put in an ice-cream machine and churn until frozen, or freeze in a shallow container, stirring every half hour or so.

92 Marmalade ice cream

500g Marmalade (see Recipe I 17) • I litre Double cream • 275ml Milk • 9 Egg yolks • 200g Caster sugar

Follow the instructions for making vanilla ice cream (see Recipe 70), until the mixture is cool.

Pour the cold custard into an ice-cream machine and churn for 6 minutes or until it begins to freeze. Add half the marmalade and churn for a further 6-8 minutes to incorporate the marmalade thoroughly into the custard. Finally add the remaining marmalade and churn briefly just to combine and solidify the ice cream.

If you do not have a machine, freeze the mixture until on the point of setting, then stir in all the marmalade and return to the freezer until solid.

93 Apricot jam ice cream

500g Apricot Jam (see Recipe 116) • 450ml Milk • 1.75 litres Double cream • 15 Egg yolks • 200g Caster sugar • 125ml Brandy

Follow the instructions for making vanilla ice cream (see Recipe 70), until the mixture is cool.

Pour the custard into an ice-cream machine and churn until it begins to freeze. Stir the brandy into the apricot jam and add half of this to the cream. Churn to incorporate the jam thoroughly into the custard. Finally add the remaining jam and churn briefly just to combine and solidify the ice cream.

If you do not have a machine, freeze the mixture until on the point of setting, then stir in all the jam and return to the freezer until solid.

CHAPTER SIX
SIX
SORBETS

94 Lemon sorbet

Serves 10

*4 Lemons, cut into quarters • 1kg Caster sugar •
5 Ripe bananas, peeled • 2 litres Fresh lemon juice*

Place the lemons, sugar and bananas in a food
processor (it is easier to do this in 2 batches) and
pulse until the mixture is coarse, with very small bits
of lemon peel still visible.

Pour into an ice-cream machine and churn until
frozen, or freeze in a suitable container.

95 Blood orange sorbet

15 Blood oranges • Caster sugar • 2 Lemons

Juice all but one of the oranges and measure the
volume of liquid. Use half that volume of caster sugar.

Cut the lemons and the remaining orange into
quarters, removing the pips. Place in a food processor
or blender with the sugar and pulse-chop to a liquid.
Add the orange juice and pulse once or twice.

Pour into an ice-cream machine and churn until
frozen, or freeze in a suitable container.

96 Pomegranate sorbet

Serves 8

10 Ripe pomegranates, squeezed and strained to make 1 litre juice • 200g Caster sugar • Juice of 2 oranges • 65ml Bitter Campari

Stir the sugar into the orange juice, then add the pomegranate juice. Taste for sweetness. Add the Campari and stir well to make sure the sugar has completely dissolved.

Pour into an ice-cream machine and churn until frozen, or freeze in a suitable container.

97 Cherry sorbet

1.5kg Cherries, stoned • 600g Caster sugar • 250ml Rosé wine

Put the cherries in a food processor with the sugar and pulse-chop to a purée. Add the wine.

Pour into an ice-cream machine and churn until frozen, or freeze in a suitable container.

Pomegranate sorbet (Recipe 96)

98 Peach and cream sorbet

8 Peaches, peeled, stoned and chopped • 150ml Double cream • Juice and finely grated zest of 1 lemon • 200g Caster sugar

Combine the peaches and lemon juice and zest with the sugar and leave for half an hour.

Stir in the cream. Pour into an ice-cream machine and churn until frozen, or freeze in a suitable container.

99 Red wine sorbet

500g Strawberries • 4 tbs Caster sugar

Sorbet
1 litre Valpolicella • 100g Caster sugar • 10 White peppercorns • 6 Whole cloves • Finely grated zest of 2 oranges

Put the wine, sugar, white pepper, cloves and orange zest into a non-reactive saucepan and boil until reduced by half. Cool, then strain. Pour into an ice-cream machine and churn until frozen, or freeze in a suitable container.

Roughly chop the strawberries and mix with the caster sugar. Place in individual bowls and cover with the sorbet.

100 Peach and lemon sorbet

8 Peaches • 250g Caster sugar • 80ml Lemon juice

Blanch the peaches in just enough water to cover. Remove the peaches from the liquid, reserving the liquid. Peel the peaches, then cut into quarters, removing the stones.

Boil the peach blanching water until it is reduced to 200ml. Add the sugar, stir until dissolved, then boil to form a syrup. Put the peaches in a food processor and blend to a coarse purée. Mix with the syrup and lemon juice.

Pour into an ice-cream machine and churn until frozen, or freeze in a suitable container.

101 Melon and lemon sorbet

5 Very ripe Cavaillon melons, seeds removed • 120ml Lemon juice • 200g Caster sugar • 125ml Water

Scoop out the flesh from the melons. Pulse-chop to a coarse texture in a food processor, then place in a bowl.

Heat the sugar gently with the water until dissolved, then boil briefly until you have a light syrup. Cool, then add to the melon along with the lemon juice. Pour into an ice-cream machine and churn until frozen, or freeze in a suitable container.

102 Blackberry sorbet

*500g Blackberries • 350g Caster sugar • Juice of
½ lemon*

Heat the sugar gently with 150ml water until dissolved,
then boil until reduced to a thick syrup. Leave to cool.

Pulse the blackberries in a food processor. Add the
syrup and lemon juice. Pour into an ice-cream
machine and churn until frozen, or freeze in a suitable
container.

103 Strawberry sorbet

Serves 8

*1.8kg Strawberries, hulled • 4 Lemons • 800-900g
Caster sugar*

Roughly chop 2 of the lemons, removing the pips, and
put them into a food processor or blender with the
sugar. Pulse-chop until the lemon and sugar have
combined. Pour into a bowl.

Purée the strawberries and add to the lemon
mixture. Squeeze the juice from the remaining
lemons and add about half of it to the purée.
Taste and add more if necessary – the flavour of the
lemon should be intense but not overpower the
strawberries.

Pour into an ice-cream machine and churn until
frozen, or freeze in a suitable container.

104 Raspberry sorbet

800g Raspberries • 2 Lemons • 350-400g Caster sugar (depending on how sweet the raspberries are)

Cut 1 lemon into 1cm pieces and remove the pips. Put the pieces into a food processor with the caster sugar and blend until the lemon and sugar have combined to a thick purée; little pieces of lemon skin should still be visible. Add the raspberries and continue to blend until combined. Add the juice of half the remaining lemon, taste and add more if necessary. The lemon flavour should be intense but not overpower the raspberries.

Pour into an ice-cream machine and churn until frozen, or freeze in a suitable container.

105 Raspberry and red wine sorbet

Serves 10

900g Raspberries • 250ml Valpolicella • Juice of ½ lemon • 100g Caster sugar • 50ml Double cream

Place all the ingredients in a food processor or blender and pulse-chop to a liquid.

Pour into an ice-cream machine and churn until frozen, or freeze in a suitable container.

106 Pear and grappa sorbet

Serves 10

1.8kg Comice or Williams pears, peeled, quartered and cored • 150ml Grappa • 2 tbs Caster sugar • 1 Vanilla pod, split lengthways • Juice of 2 lemons

Put the pears in a pan with the sugar, vanilla pod and 250ml water and cook until soft. Drain. Add the grappa and lemon juice. Push through a very fine sieve, then leave to cool.

Pour into an ice-cream machine and churn until frozen, or freeze in a suitable container.

107 Campari sorbet

Serves 10

200ml Campari • 1 litre Grapefruit juice • 400g Caster sugar • Juice of 2 lemons • Juice of 2 oranges

Whisk together the grapefruit juice and sugar. Add the Campari and the lemon and orange juice.

Pour into an ice-cream machine and churn until frozen, or freeze in a suitable container.

108 Fig sorbet

12 Black figs, very ripe • Juice of 1 lemon • 200g Caster sugar • 150ml Double cream

Peel the figs, leaving some skin on. Put them in a food processor with the lemon juice and chop coarsely. Put in a bowl and stir in the sugar and the cream.

Pour into an ice-cream machine and churn until frozen, or freeze in a suitable container.

109 Mascarpone sorbet

Serves 6

250g Mascarpone • 270g Caster sugar • Juice of 1 lemon

Heat the sugar gently with 350ml water until dissolved, then boil briefly until you have a light syrup. Add the lemon juice and leave to cool.

Put the mascarpone into a bowl and stir with a whisk to lighten. Stir in the cooled syrup. Pour into an ice-cream machine and churn until frozen, or freeze in a suitable container.

110 Chocolate sorbet

Serves 8

150g Cocoa powder • 250g Caster sugar • 100ml Vecchia Romagna brandy

Heat the sugar gently with 750ml water until dissolved, then boil briefly until you have a light syrup. Add the cocoa powder. Cook gently, stirring from time to time, for 15-20 minutes, until the cocoa powder is completely dissolved. Strain, cool and then add the brandy.

Pour into an ice-cream machine and churn until frozen, or freeze in a suitable container.

111 Chocolate coffee sorbet

Serves 8

150g Cocoa powder • 150ml Strong coffee • 250g Caster sugar

Bring 650ml water to the boil with the sugar and boil for 4 minutes. Allow to cool. Add the coffee and cocoa powder and cook over a low heat for 15 minutes, stirring to combine. Strain.

Pour into an ice-cream machine and churn until frozen, or freeze in a suitable container.

112 Vanilla and chocolate sorbet

Serves 8

2 Vanilla pods, cut into 2cm lengths • 150g Cocoa powder • 250g Caster sugar • 100ml Amaretto liqueur • 2 tsp Vanilla essence

Place the vanilla pods in a food processor and process to a fine powder. Mix with the sugar.

Dissolve the vanilla sugar in 750ml water over a medium heat. Bring slowly to the boil, then add the cocoa powder, stirring. Reduce the heat and simmer for 25 minutes. Cool, then stir in the Amaretto and vanilla essence.

Pour into an ice-cream machine and churn until frozen, or freeze in a suitable container.

113 Lemon granita

250ml Lemon juice • Finely grated zest of 1 lemon • 100g Caster sugar

In a heavy-bottomed saucepan, bring 500ml water and the sugar to the boil. Cook until reduced by almost half. Remove from the heat and cool, then add the lemon juice and zest.

Pour into shallow ice trays or cake tins and put in the freezer. Allow the liquid to freeze partially, about 20-30 minutes. Mash with a fork to break up the ice crystals, then return to the freezer and leave for »

« a further 20 minutes. Repeat this process, mashing up the frozen liquid, then returning it to the freezer and freezing, until you have a hard, dry, crystalline granita.

---

114 Strawberry granita

500g Strawberries • 200g Caster sugar • 1 tbs Balsamic vinegar • Juice of 1 lemon

Heat 150g of the sugar gently with 150ml water until dissolved, then boil briefly until you have a light syrup. Cool and add the vinegar.

With a fork, smash the strawberries with the remaining sugar. Add the lemon juice and mix with the syrup. Churn in an ice-cream machine or freeze in a shallow container, stirring every half hour or so.

Pour the liquid into shallow ice trays or cake tins and put in the freezer. Allow the juice to freeze partially, about 20-30 minutes. Mash with a fork to break up the ice crystals, then return to the freezer and leave for a further 20 minutes. Repeat this process, mashing up the frozen juice, returning to the freezer and freezing, until you have a hard, dry, crystalline granita. This takes up to 2½ hours. Serve with crème fraîche.

115 Coffee granita

650ml Espresso coffee • 200g Caster sugar

Dissolve the sugar in the hot coffee. Allow to cool. Test for sweetness and strength, adding a little water if too strong.

Pour the liquid into shallow ice trays or cake tins and put in the freezer. Allow the coffee to freeze partially, about 20-30 minutes. Mash with a fork to break up the ice crystals, then return to the freezer and leave for a further 20 minutes. Repeat this process, mashing up the frozen coffee, returning to the freezer and freezing, until you have a hard, dry, crystalline granita. This takes up to 2½ hours. Use immediately. Serve with crème fraîche.

CHAPTER
SEVEN
JAMS

116 Apricot and nectarine jam

Makes about 1kg

1kg Very ripe, dark-coloured apricots, stoned weight (keep the stones) • 4 Ripe nectarines, peeled and stoned • 500g Caster sugar

Crack the apricot stones open and remove the kernels. Blanch for 30 seconds in boiling water, then cool a little and peel. Reserve.

Put the apricots, sugar and 120ml water into a large, thick-bottomed saucepan. Heat very gently, stirring until the sugar dissolves and the juices flow from the apricots. Raise the heat slightly, add the nectarines and boil, stirring. The fruit will break down and the liquid will evaporate.

The jam is ready when the steam rising from the pan is less dense and the surface begins to seethe rather than bubble. This will take about 25-30 minutes, depending on how ripe the apricots are. Test for setting point by placing a spoonful of the jam on a cold plate. If the jam runs very slowly, it is ready. Finally, stir in the apricot kernels. Spoon the jam into sterilised jars and seal. Store in a cool, dark place.

117 Marmalade

We have given no quantities as the recipe works in proportion of fruit to sugar.

Seville oranges • Caster sugar

Soak the oranges in cold water for 24-48 hours so the skins soften and expand, then drain and rinse.

Fill a large, thick-bottomed saucepan with the oranges, cover with cold water and slowly bring to the boil. Reduce the heat, cover with the lid askew and simmer very gently for 3-4 hours, stirring from time to time, until the oranges are completely soft. Make sure that the liquid does not totally evaporate during the cooking; add a drop more water if it does. Remove from the heat and cool.

Take the soft oranges out of the pan and put the pan and any remaining juices to one side. Cut each orange in half and remove the pips and any tough fibres. Roughly cut the flesh and skin into 1cm pieces. Weigh this orange pulp, then return it to the saucepan.

Measure out two-thirds of the orange pulp's weight in caster sugar. Add the sugar to the saucepan, return to the heat and gently bring to the boil, stirring to prevent sticking and to dissolve the sugar. Turn the heat down and simmer for 30 minutes. The marmalade should be very dense and dark in colour.

Test for setting by placing a spoonful of the marmalade on a cold plate. If the marmalade runs very slowly, it is ready. Cool for 5 minutes, then put into sterilised jars and seal. Store in a cool, dark place.

Marmalade (Recipe 117) and Roasted raspberry jam (Recipe 118)

118 Roasted raspberry jam

Makes about 5kg

3kg Very ripe raspberries • 2.5kg Caster sugar

Preheat the oven to 200°C/Gas Mark 6.

Place the raspberries in a heatproof dish. Do the same with the sugar. Bake both in the preheated oven until very hot, about half an hour. The raspberries will sweat but will not totally collapse.

Combine the hot sugar and hot raspberries and stir together. The raspberries will melt with the sugar and become instant jam. Cool.

Put into sterilised jam jars and seal. Store in a cool, dark place.

119 Quince cheese

Quinces • Caster sugar

Preheat the oven to 150°C/Gas Mark 2.

Rub the quinces with a large cloth to remove the down. Put them on a baking tray whole (or halved if they are very large), cover with foil and bake for about 1 1/2 hours, until they are soft but the skins remain unbroken; the time will vary according to the size of the quinces.

Remove from the oven, allow to cool until they can be easily handled, then cut in half, if necessary, and take out the core and any tough pieces. Push the flesh and skin through a vegetable mill.

Weigh the pulp and put an equal amount of caster sugar into a saucepan. Add the quince pulp and bring to the boil. Cook, stirring constantly, until the mixture darkens in colour and comes away from the sides of the pan. This could take up to half an hour.

When ready, pour out onto a large flat, cold plate and leave to set.

Index

The authors would like to thank Tanya Nathan, Ronnie Bonnetti, Fiona MacIntyre, Imogen Fortes, Sarah Lavelle, David Loftus and Mark Porter, and all the staff at the River Cafe.

1 3 5 7 9 10 8 6 4 2

Text © Rose Gray and Ruth Rogers 2006

First published in the United Kingdom in 2006 by Ebury Press, an imprint of Ebury Publishing, Random House UK Ltd., 20 Vauxhall Bridge Road, London SW1V 2SA

Random House Australia (Pty) Limited, 20 Alfred Street, Milsons Point, Sydney, New South Wales 2061, Australia

Random House New Zealand Limited, 18 Poland Road, Glenfield, Auckland 10, New Zealand

Random House (Pty) Limited, Isle of Houghton Corner of Boundary Road & Carse O'Gowrie Houghton, 2198, South Africa

Random House Publishers India Private Limited, 301 World Trade Tower, Hotel Intercontinental Grand Complex, Barakhamba Lane, New Delhi 110 001, India

Random House UK Limited Reg. No. 954009, www.randomhouse.co.uk

Papers used by Ebury Press are natural, recyclable products made from wood grown in sustainable forests.

A CIP catalogue record is available for this book from the British Library.

ISBN: 009191437X   ISBN: 9780091914370 (from Jan 2007)

Printed and bound in Italy by Graphicom SRL

Designed by Mark Porter Design, www.markporter.com

Copies are available at special rates for bulk orders. Contact the sales development team on 020 7840 8487 or visit www.booksforpromotions.co.uk for more information.